# Finish the

MW01104568

*what you need to know to establish*
*a healthy youth ministry in your setting*

Mark Schaufler Copyright 2005

ISBN 1-886904-36-7
Library of Congress Control Number 2004117419

Published by MST Ministries
P.O. Box 8490 Lacey WA 98509
Phone 360-456-5624
Fax 360-438-9058
www.mstgo.com
www.finish-the-race.org

"Scripture taken from the
HOLY BIBLE:
NEW INTERNATIONAL VERSION.
Copyright 1973, 1978, 1984
By International Bible Society.
Used by permission of Zondervan Bible Publishers."

Printed in the United States by Morris Publishing
3212 E. Hwy 30 Kearney, NE 68847
800-650-7888

# Table of Contents

# Foreword and Forewarned

September 1980- We began to work with a large youth ministry (two hundred students in their high school ministry pool) as volunteers. Our role was to lead a group of fourteen sophomore girls on Sunday mornings. It was a good introduction to youth ministry, and I learned some key principles that would help me later.

October 1982- I was given the reins of a non-existent youth ministry in a new church meeting in the basement of a daycare. After working my construction job, I gave youth ministry the ten hours a week I had left.

Somewhere in the first two years of establishing that youth ministry I had a God experience that has determined the heart beat of my life ever since. I was praying for the students and noting how messed up their home situations were. One set of students had an alcoholic dad, another a man living with their mom. One student resembled a cross between Dracula and the hunchback of Notre Dame, and then there were the kids whose mom had married the neighbor who had been sexually abusing them.

At one point God clearly spoke to me, "Fight for them". I said, "What?" He repeated, "Fight for them, nobody else is". Ten years later, it was a healthy youth ministry with thirty-five volunteer staff and over two hundred students in our ministry pool. When I left, one of our youth staff took my place and continued the fight in that location.

That was a long time ago now (1992). When I'm offered a ministry position I have to ask, "Can I minister from that position better than I can now?" That has led me to minister as an evangelist, adjunct youth ministry college professor, overseas youth ministry trainer, author, seminar and conference speaker, motivational school speaker, short term mission team leader, and all in any given year. I have also focused in a couple of locations long enough to start other youth ministries.

February 10, 1999, was the kick-off service for a new youth ministry that would begin with students and leaders from three small area churches meeting in one of the churches' basement. I was already heavily involved in ministry worldwide and could only give an average of five hours a week to the venture.

Now, it is a healthy youth ministry (with a pool of about fifty students), with volunteer leadership raised up from that original group of students and leaders. For the first two years, I was the key individual but as leadership was raised up I drifted back into the shadows. Now I am just the honored periodic guest.

As we entered into 2004, I began working with another youth ministry. It's about an hour from my home and we have already begun training volunteers. They've done their homework and are now holding youth services with a growing number of students.

Maybe you're like me when this all began. You have been given little to work with and not much help. Welcome to "The Unknown Race". Don't feel alone. Most youth ministries are like yours. There are some that look like ours did "after ten years" but most, I repeat, most aren't. The average church size in American is less than one hundred and that is partially due to the lack of healthy youth ministries.

In this book, you will get the principles (guiding wisdom) and practices (tools and methods) to establish a healthy youth ministry on the limited amounts of time that you have to offer. Even if you are a full time, paid, youth worker you don't have enough time to do everything that needs to be done. All of us have to learn how to make our time count with students and staff.

As the pages unfold, you will find help. It will require work and most likely little thanks from those around you. Even the students you minister to will not say thanks. But in time (don't measure it in days or months but years), you will see students who are pastors, missionaries, youth pastors, and solid people in their churches.

Now I often get daily reminders of why we did what we did in those early years. It comes through those former students and the lives they now live because somebody took the time and effort to work with them.

There is a training path that everyone must take to be a leader involved in a healthy Youth Ministry. It is dependent on your proficiency in five levels of youth ministry.


Here are the five levels:
- Bible
- Background
- Basics
- Building Blocks
- Bonus Opportunities

Working with students, your <u>Bible</u> knowledge will be taxed and tested by them. This is the first level of training. They will ask every question there is, and then some, as you begin to spend time with them and their friends.

We live in a very spiritual age where information and misinformation is readily available to almost anyone. You can't get by on the information that you have heard growing up, listening to sermons. At some point, you will need to really know your Bible.

It doesn't mean you know everything off the top of your head but that you can find everything when needed. Life is an open book test; know where to find what you need. To help you evaluate this first level we have created a Bible Proficiency Test that you can take. It is an open book test and can be downloaded from our <u>www.finish-the-race.org</u> site. There are also several avenues of study you can pursue if that area needs some additional help.

Next are the <u>Background</u> issues. These will be covered in this text.

- What is a teenager?
- How do they learn?
- How do they change?
- What are the facts we need to take into account to minister to them?
- What does a healthy youth ministry look like?

Understanding these will allow us to effectively pursue level number three: <u>Basics</u>. How can your Sunday school, mid-week meeting, retreat, or event help promote a healthy youth ministry? The Basic issues will be covered in this text.

<u>Building Blocks</u> (level four) allow you to work from your solid foundation and grow. Now you pass on what you have learned to additional staff. As you train them, you can expand into new areas of ministry and work with some of the other opportunities in the youth ministry world. We will also cover these areas and reference you to some great books that have additional material.

<u>Bonus Opportunities</u> only come after you have established yourself in your church and community with a foundation of credibility and faithfulness over an extended period, usually at least two years. We will cover these areas and reference you to some great books that have additional materials on these issues.

Understanding the track will enable you to spend your time where it matters. My youngest daughter runs cross-country in high school. Before they run a race, they walk the course. Then they know where the turns are and which is the right way to go. Missing a turn can cost the team a race.

Rushing ahead to Building Blocks or Bonus Opportunities could be a costly mistake in youth ministry. Take the time to master each level so that you are a part of establishing something that will be healthy and produce the disciples Christ called us to make.

# 1 The First Aid Kit and Common Ailments

I'm not sure which New Testament church you are privileged to be a part of: Crete had liars, evil brutes, and lazy gluttons. Corinth had lawsuits between the believers and a man sleeping with his father's wife. You get the picture; no satire, our salvation is a privilege. But if you have an illusion of what the church will be like you are destined for trouble and a short stay in the church.

The church is a collection of real people trying to follow Jesus and those that are there for dozens of other reasons. It is always becoming His bride but never attaining that status because it is always adding more, raw, real people. Having real people means you need a real First Aid Kit to deal with the real wounds that happen. Whether it's words, actions, inaction, or someone's careless sword (part of the armor we all get), it all hurts.

Being involved in ministry means you will be shot at, wounded with words, and misunderstood to an even greater degree. In military terms, it is called "friendly fire."

People within the church will do all of this. Sometimes it will be accidental, often unintentional, and periodically very calculated. No matter, you must stay healthy despite the pain. If you can learn how to turn wounds into scars, you will have mastered a skill that you need to pass on to your students so that they can survive their own "friendly fire."

As you minister, you will make a few mistakes that deserve some criticism. Through misunderstanding you may be called a cult leader or fanatic.

Spiritually, you also have an enemy who will shoot his best ammunition at you as well. Get used to it. You minister in a war zone.

*In addition to all this, take up the shield of faith, with which you can extinguish all the flaming arrows of the evil one. Ephesians 6:16*

Those who don't learn how to use the First Aid Kit become victims and casualties. Over seventy-five percent of all people who begin in ministry are not involved five years later. Of those who make it through the first five years, eighty percent of them will be in ministry for the rest of their lives. The difference? Ideal settings? No, guess who learned how to use the First Aid Kit.

Here is the strategy for basic first aid in ministry and life in general. First, acknowledge the pain. "I'm okay" doesn't work in real life if you aren't okay. Pain is there to help modify your behavior, and if you learn from it, make your future different.

*No discipline seems pleasant at the time, but painful. Later on, however, it produces a harvest of righteousness and peace for those who have been trained by it. Hebrews 12:11*

Next, determine why it hurts.

- Did you hurt someone and they lashed back?
- Did someone try to help you and you resisted so it hurt because they held you tightly while you fought them?
- Did someone use words that weren't true, yet applied them to you?
- Was someone evil and you were too close when they did their evil action?
- Was your pride injured?

How it happened and what part of you is hurt will determine what you need to do next.

Ask for forgiveness from Father God for your part in it (if you have any), and those you hurt. If you are just a victim, then spend time in God's presence so He can be the God of all comfort and flush out the wound's poison.

*If we confess our sins, he is faithful and just and will forgive us our sins and purify us from all unrighteousness. 1 John 1:9*

*Therefore, if you are offering your gift at the altar and there remember that your brother has something against you, leave your gift there in front of the altar. First go and be reconciled to your brother; then come and offer your gift. Matthew 5:23-24*

*Praise be to the God and Father of our Lord Jesus Christ, the Father of compassion and the God of all comfort, who comforts us in all our troubles, so that we can comfort those in any trouble with the comfort we ourselves have received from God. 2 Corinthians 1:3-4*

If it just hurts because it was a painful lesson, learn from it. Get something from the Bible that will give you a different strategy for the same kind of event in the future.

*Do not conform any longer to the pattern of this world, but be transformed by the renewing of your mind. Then you will be able to test and approve what God's will is—his good, pleasing and perfect will. Romans 12:2*

Now keep the wound clean. Don't let the words or action happen again, if possible. Don't let the previous wound be re-lived and you become re-injured. That may mean you do something different than before. It may mean you need to talk to someone about what they did to you.

*If your brother sins against you, go and show him his fault, just between the two of you. If he listens to you, you have won your brother over. Matthew 18:15*

Pray for those who did the wounding. If they become a nightmare or a nagging thought, you won't heal.

*You have heard that it was said, 'Love your neighbor and hate your enemy.' But I tell you: Love your enemies and pray for those who persecute you, that you may be sons of your Father in Heaven. He causes his sun to rise on the evil and the good, and sends rain on the righteous and the unrighteous.* Matthew *5:43-45*

Praying for them will also disarm any strategies the roaring lion has to divide and conquer within the family of God.

*If you have forgiven anyone, I also forgive him. And what I have forgiven—if there was anything to forgive—I have forgiven in the sight of Christ for your sake, in order that Satan might not outwit us. For we are not unaware of his schemes.* 2 Corinthians *2:10-11.*

If it is bigger than what you can do by yourself, (you and God), get some help. Seek out advice and counsel from someone who knows how to use the First Aid Kit. Don't go to someone who will pour salt on the wound and make you madder or re-injure you.

*Is any one of you in trouble? He should pray. Is anyone happy? Let him sing songs of praise. Is any one of you sick? He should call on the elders of the church to pray over him and anoint him with oil in the name of the Lord. And the prayer offered in faith will make the sick person well; the Lord will raise him up. If he has sinned, he will be forgiven. Therefore confess your sins to each other and pray for each other so that you may be healed. The prayer of a righteous man is powerful and effective.* James *5:13-16*

Just sitting around and hoping you get better won't work either. Moving forward with a scriptural response will get you back sooner and stronger than before.

*Therefore, strengthen your feeble arms and weak knees. "Make level paths for your feet," so that the lame may not be disabled, but rather healed. Hebrews 12:12-13*

In your First Aid Kit, you need several things. You need wisdom from the Scriptures so you can explain the unpleasant events of life to your students and yourself. Following Jesus guarantees trouble. If you or your students think following Jesus makes life easy you will be in for some unpleasant surprises. Remember, we live in a war zone not an amusement park.

*In fact, everyone who wants to live a godly life in Christ Jesus will be persecuted, 2 Timothy 3:12*

*Be self-controlled and alert. Your enemy the devil prowls around like a roaring lion looking for someone to devour. Resist him, standing firm in the faith, because you know that your brothers throughout the world are undergoing the same kind of sufferings. 1 Peter 5:8-9*

Forgiveness needs to be in a big bottle. You will need to give it out and receive it. As people are doing things for God, it will bring out the best and the worst in everyone. Learning to forgive must happen quickly and continuously when, not if, someone is hurt. It is the 911 of life. Without it, you will divide and scatter instead of build and unify.

Patience comes in big economy bottles; get three. Nothing good comes easily or quickly. Details never fall into place; people aren't home when you call; promises aren't kept;

and expectations are seldom met. Our opportunity to grow while we work for Father God is a promise. Once you have mastered an area and it begins to work for you then He will challenge you to a new one. Keep patience well stocked.

Get seven packages of prayer as well, one for each day of the week. You will need them and a new set of packages each week. You will need to pray for help and wisdom and for those who have hurt you.

Apply prayer to yourself on a daily basis and as often as you see the need in your group. No one is exempt from wounds. Your leaders, parents, students, and church staff all bleed. Be ready with the kit. No one gets better without treatment. Offer the treatment even if people are reluctant to show you the wound. Often you can see the wound before they will admit they have one.

Over the years I have collected my share of wounds. Today they are just scars and stories. I can laugh about them, cry, or teach a valuable lesson. I don't limp, avoid certain people, or locations. There are no wounds that change my behavior or capacity because they are all scars. If you don't treat them they can become ministry-ending injuries of tragic proportions. I know too many people who haven't finished the race because of their wounds.

Here are some scenarios that just might happen to you or people you know. They have all happened to me. With each one is a treatment strategy that can enable you to properly treat the wounds. Through these scenarios I hope you will learn to:

- clean it out
- keep it clean

- if it is bigger than what you can handle by yourself, get some help.

One night after a church service I went over to meet a visitor to the church. He was in his late fifties or early sixties and we shook hands. It was an awkward shake because he only had a thumb and one full finger on that hand. After a couple of questions, he let me know that he had lost the fingers to save his hand.

He had neglected a small sliver in one of his fingers. It had become infected and had gone to blood poisoning before he did anything about it. In time, gangrene had set in and the awkward handshake was the ultimate result. Learn to use your First Aid Kit. Don't let pride or busyness get in the way.

**Scenario One**

You lose a thousand dollars on a winter retreat because several churches that had promised to come, back out at the last minute. You still have to pay the camp the minimum amount promised in the contract. Church finances are very tight, and the board decides that you need to go to the other churches that were involved and get the money from them.

- Clean it out- Sit down and figure out what went wrong with the finances. Maybe the church board imposed some restrictions on you that forced the crisis. Maybe you blew it. Either way, see where the fault lies. If it lies with them, write out an explanation for the finances. Submit it respectively to them and see if there is a response. If it is just your fault, write out an explanation and respectively submit it to them documenting how you could correct the problem next time. Take into account how often this kind of thing has happened in the past as well.

- Keep it clean- Pray for them no matter what kind of interaction you have with them. Prepare for the reduction in pay or payback. Don't talk bad about them to anyone or feed anyone's anger (your spouse or your students). When thoughts about the situation or people arise, take them as a prompting to pray, fight in the spirit world, not in the flesh.

- Get some help- You should have a mentor, board member, or significant person who you can talk to. If no one exists locally, most denominations have someone you can talk to. When you talk to them, don't present a case for your feelings or frustration. Instead, share with them your struggle in trying to deal with it. Allow them to ask questions or contact the pastor if needed to get the whole picture on the issue.

## Scenario Two

On your first mission trip, rumors are generated while you are gone that discredit the trip's ministry and years of work in that church. The parents are very upset at you before you know anything about the rumors. You return home to very angry parents who destroy what good the trip had accomplished.

- Clean it out- With a good attitude, you do your homework so that you know what is really being said and by whom. Send a report of what happened from your perspective for the whole trip, not just a defense of your actions versus their understanding, so that the purpose and accomplishments are not lost in the rumors. Apologize for the things that did happen and ask forgiveness if someone is upset with you even without just cause (Matthew 5:23-24).

- Keep it clean- Pray for those who may have become your adversaries (Matthew 5:43-48).

- Get some help- Work closely with your senior pastor and keep things open with him. Document everything that you can, and find the process that started the problem. Make the necessary changes to correct the problem for next time. For us, that meant a "No News is Good News" policy. No one calls home unless it is necessary.

- Get ready to go again the next year and deal with the baggage from the previous year.

## Scenario Three

Some rumors surface that you are having an illicit relationship with one of the students in your group.

- Clean it out- Try to find out why this rumor could exist, spending a lot of time with one person or they seem to get all the advantages of a special relationship, etc. Ask your spouse or someone else if there might be something going on in the student's mind that you are unaware of. We can be blind to this kind of stuff. Don't get defensive.

- Keep it clean- Pray for the people and make any adjustments that you need to eliminate the fuel for the rumor fire. Contact the rumor person, if appropriate or identified, with the full knowledge of the senior pastor.

- Get some help- Keep this and all steps you take in the full knowledge of the senior pastor. If he was the one who alerted you to the rumor, then work with him, don't react to him. If it doesn't seem to resolve in this way, talk to denominational leadership.

**Scenario Four**

Your church board is ready to rebel against the leadership over the color of the carpet. They want your support for their actions.

- Clean it out- Listen, but then remind them of the scriptural principles that they are potentially violating (David and Saul). If there are some issues that do need to be addressed by the senior pastor then help them formulate a way to do it. Keep the senior pastor informed at all times and let them know that you are on his team.

- Keep it clean- Don't let their words poison your heart. Pray for them and the issues involved. If there are some additional ways to deal with the issue and you can be the peacemaker, feel free to do it without betraying the senior pastor or subverting him.

- Get some help - If it is getting out of control talk to whatever boards and groups exist within the leadership of the church with your pastor's permission. Don't go beyond that unless there are scriptural violations. Opinions aren't right or wrong; it is how you deal with them that can be.

**Scenario Five**

You need some funds for basic youth ministry materials; curriculum, training seminars, classroom aids, etc., but those that were promised disappear into the latest building project funds.

- Clean it out- Investigate the real issue not just what you have "heard". If it is true, ask what policies have changed or if there is some information you are not aware of, i.e. the church is broke. Don't demand your "rights", but deal with the changing situation.

- Keep it clean- Pray for people that come to mind if you find yourself getting upset at the situation. Come up with other ways to raise the money or meet the needs of the ministry.

- Get some help- Talk to others who can help you accomplish the results without poisoning them with your words. Don't throw your poison around. Deal with it.

If you have enjoyed these non-threatening tests you can get more at our website www.finish-the-race.org. Look for first aid scenarios.

# Worry; the other Health Thief

*The one who received the seed that fell among the thorns is the man who hears the word, but the worries of this life and the deceitfulness of wealth choke it, making it unfruitful.* Matthew 13:22

*Who of you by worrying can add a single hour to his life?* Matthew 6:27

Today we call it stress. For this "new" society foe, we have prescriptions, books, managers, and websites. Jesus called it worry and warned us of it.

In ministry, as in any part of the life Jesus calls us to live, we have a choice on how we respond. If we choose the worry route, we will become choked and unfruitful. Chances are one of the many diseases that find their cause in a worry-laden body, will shorten our lives as well.

Worry happens when we view our circumstances through our eyes and not Father God's. As a result we find ourselves in actions that are counterproductive; ie. panic, or paralyzed by fear. We must learn how to respond in His way to bear the fruit of His Spirit.

For example, if you find yourself worrying about an upcoming event, you may need to be taking some course of action to deal with an issue for that event instead.

If you have a student who isn't doing well and you worry about them, instead, pray for them or do something to help them out. Worry accomplishes nothing but it can destroy the opportunity for great things.

Whatever causes us to worry needs to be seen as a call to action, not the negative reaction of worry.

*Peace I leave with you; my peace I give you. I do not give to you as the world gives. Do not let your hearts be troubled and do not be afraid. John 14:27*

*I have told you these things, so that in me you may have peace. In this world you will have trouble. But take heart! I have overcome the world. John 16:33*

*Come to me, all you who are weary and burdened, and I will give you rest. Take my yoke upon you and learn from me, for I am gentle and humble in heart, and you will find rest for your souls. For my yoke is easy and my burden is light. Matthew 11:28-30*

Internal peace needs to be our normal state despite the conditions around us. If it is, we can respond properly, with His help and guidance. If fear, trouble, and worry consistently characterize our lives we are missing something in our relationship with Jesus.

Find, keep, and maintain the peace that Christ talks about. It may mean some extra time in prayer, releasing the "yoke" that you are carrying so you can take His, or slowing down. Peace isn't a nice option, it is essential. Without it, your spiritual and physical health will be short lived. With it, you can look forward to the years ahead of you, knowing that there will be fruit from your labors as you and He carry the yoke together.

# The Poison of Pride

*Pride goes before destruction and a haughty spirit before a fall. Proverbs 16:18*

*Young men, in the same way be submissive to those who are older. All of you, clothe yourselves with humility toward one another, because, "God opposes the proud but gives grace to the humble." 2 Peter 5:5 and Proverbs 3:34*

Unfortunately, this poison has eliminated many a youth worker from the ministry field. Its deadliness is often overlooked because of the variety of symptoms it can have. We value some of them and yet they are still destined for destruction and God's opposition.

- Hard work can disguise the pride of not wanting to ask for help.
- Arguing your point because you are sure you are right can appear as confidence or wisdom but it can hide your arrogance towards others as well.
- Leadership vision can cover the insecurities that people have as everyone needs to get on board your vision train. Anyone going a different direction is a rebel. In truth, you can be the rebel and they are trying to keep you on track.
- You leave to go to a "higher calling" because you couldn't stay and clean up the messes you have made. It can appear noble, but it will only produce the same mess that you are moving away from.
- You make a good first impression, but from that point on, your actions only detract from that impression. You have

to constantly have new people around you to "wow" them with your first impression.

- You aren't teachable because you are an expert in the field due to your extensive reading and past experience. Unfortunately, most of us saw the same commercial and read the newspaper article that you are basing your expertise on.

- You hide behind your title, which some would see as respect. Instead of realizing that respect is earned not demanded, the insecure youth worker will make every effort to use and see that the title is used whenever possible.

Who wouldn't want a hard working, confident, well trained, vision casting leader to carry the youth ministry to the next level? Father God, for one, if the source of all these characteristics is pride.

To be all we need to be, we need to stay connected to our vine, Jesus. Interacting with Him in prayer and study won't allow us to have these characteristics (pride) for long.

*Humble yourselves, therefore, under God's mighty hand, that he may lift you up in due time. Cast all your anxiety on him because he cares for you. 2 Peter 5:6-7*

In practical terms that means we are characterized by the following traits:

- Hard work alongside those we need with us to see God's direction fulfilled.

- Confidence in God's ability to use all of us as each has their unique part in the body.
- Leadership that see Christ as the head of the body and their leadership in submission to Jesus and His people.
- You are good at cleaning up your inevitable messes.
- Consistency and faithfulness are the key characteristics people use to describe you.
- You are teachable and are constantly trying to learn from others.
- Your title is respected by all because you have earned it based on your character and actions.

When we take the pride route, we poison the path and will eventually be forced to find another one. It may mean moving on or dropping out of youth ministry altogether. At that point, you join the list of casualties that litter the ministry path.

# Lust, Laziness, and Losing

**LUST** is a highly advertised issue and rightly so. The casualty list of those who have been victims is long and full of famous names. However, it isn't always seen for what it often is; the wrong response to other issues.

Assuming we take a simple look at it, it's just a man or woman who desires the forbidden fruit of another's sexual company. But, even then, it is not so simple. First, there are the thoughts that were not controlled. Then there is the secret time with someone. Finally, the plan and the execution.

Seldom is it ever simple. Fruitful ministry with healthy relationships doesn't leave much room or desire for an illicit relationship. Instead, there are other issues that have enhanced the look of the lustful sexual temptation.

_In the spring, at the time, when Kings go off to war._
_David sent Joab out with the King's men and the whole Israelite_
_Army. They destroyed the Ammonites and besieged Rabbah. But_
_David remained in Jerusalem. 2 Samuel 11:1_

Ministry is a spiritual battle and avoiding it doesn't make it go away. In this scripture, David avoided his warrior King role and ended up in bed with another man's wife. David's avoidance of one battle cost him the war in the area of lust. Avoiding issues, challenges, or conflict sets one up for the final fatal battle in lust.

Strained marital relationships, tension over finances, failure in an effort, can send some looking for comfort or solace in the wrong places. That can lead to a lust problem as easily as the skimpily clad model in the latest media format.

Anger can also look for ways to express itself that are seemingly less destructive than violence. Given the right opportunities, anger can end up in a lustful adventure. Instead, the problem needs to be faced and tackled.

*Consider it pure joy. my brothers, whenever you face trials of many kinds, because you know that the testing of your faith develops perseverance. Perseverance must finish its work so that you may be mature and complete, not lacking anything. James 1:2-4*

**LAZINESS** can be hidden fairly easily in a ministry setting. Phone calls, computer research, home visits, and artistic projects can be a fruitful day of ministry or hide a total waste of time.

Sometimes people in full time ministry have gone from one school setting to another and now find themselves in their first full time "job" (ministry). They may not have any kind of work ethic established in their daily routine, yet.

Utilizing our time is a constant challenge everyone faces in ministry. We need to learn to make the most of the time in ministry we do have. We also need to learn to be honest with how we use the ministry time we do have.

*Making the most of every opportunity, because the days are evil. Ephesians 5:16*

I have kept a journal during several years of ministry and it has forced me to evaluate how and what I do. It has always resulted in some adjustments of how I do ministry and use my family time. Taking the time to do the journals undoubtedly helped me be more effective in ministry and much more fruitful in my efforts as a father and husband.

**LOSING** is a reality, if you're keeping score. It is too easy to compare ourselves and our numbers with others. At that point, we have set ourselves up to lose. We also set ourselves up for losing if we have expectations that aren't based on reality. Our numbers expectations can have us quitting and packing to go despite the fact that our efforts have been very successful and fruitful.

On the other hand, if our numbers fit our expectations we can be satisfied with our results and not pursue the higher purposes and results that we could be a part of. In that sense we lose what could have been because we are content with the results based on our numbers.

If we aren't playing the number game then we can enjoy the joy of obedience that anyone can have regardless of the apparent results. Only then can we be the real winners that all of Father God's children are when we obey.

# 2 Keeping Yourself in the Race

In order to maintain your edge on the track, you will need to set the pace. Your personal challenges from the Scripture and the throne will force you to face the same issues that your students have. The stakes are higher, but you can always relate to student's struggles if you are facing your own.

*Consider it pure joy, my brothers, whenever you face trails of many kinds, because you know that the testing of your faith develops perseverance. Perseverance must finish its work so that you may be mature and complete, not lacking anything. If any of you lacks wisdom, he should ask God, who gives generously to all without finding fault, and it will be given to him. James 1:2-5*

As different as the two worlds may seem, yours and theirs, the same basic issues will still surround them. Faith, trust, mercy, grace, and faithfulness, are common areas of challenge you face as a leader as well as your students. Learn it. Pass it on.

If God challenges you to give a hundred dollars a month to missions, the students may face a hundred dollars a year challenge. If you need to talk about Jesus to your neighbor, they need to talk to the kid in the next locker. Reading and applying the Bible isn't just for them; it will challenge you, too. When God challenges you to a task He may also be giving the students in your group their next challenge.

My burden for missions became the source and inspiration for our short-term mission program. What happened in our campus ministries was partially a result of my presence on the campus. At times, you will be on the same ministry team as the students. Other times you will be their coach. Sometimes you will have to work with them from a distance. At that point, you are their manager. However, you must set and establish the pace.

Your capacity to function in those areas will be dependent on your growing relationship and knowledge of Jesus. His challenges for you will keep you on the cutting edge of your ministry. His challenges for you will help you to understand the struggles your students face as they follow Jesus and face their issues.

_But grow in the grace and knowledge of our Lord and Savior Jesus Christ. To him be glory both now and forever! Amen. 2 Peter 3:18_

_Follow my example, as I follow the example of Christ. 1 Corinthians 11:1_

It will also guarantee that you will deal with your wounds on a regular basis. If you're a walking wounded leader, you will only bleed on other people. Make sure you give Jesus the time He needs to keep you healthy.

Maintaining your growth will depend on your ability to reserve one on one time with Jesus and God's word on a daily basis. It will also depend on your ability to learn new skills and information that will help you in your ministry to students. You will contribute more to a healthy youth ministry with five hours a week if you and Jesus are on the same page than if you give the youth ministry ten hours of haphazard energy and enthusiasm.

*I am the vine; you are the branches. If a man remains in me and I in him, he will bear much fruit; apart from me you can do nothing. John 15:5*

This text is dedicated to increasing your skills and the information you need for a healthy youth ministry. You will also need your daily interaction with Jesus and the scriptures. Learn to pace yourself so that you can do what is needed first and what is possible next. Martha and Mary show us this clearly.

*As Jesus and his disciples were on their way, he came to a village where a woman named Martha opened her home to him. She had a sister called Mary, who sat at the Lord's feet listening to what he said. But Martha was distracted by all the preparations that had to be made. She came to him and asked, "Lord, don't you care that my sister has left me to do the work by myself? Tell her to help me!"*

*"Martha, Martha," the Lord answered, "you are worried and upset about many things, but only one thing is needed. Mary*

*has chosen what is better, and it will not be taken away from her." Luke 10:38-42*

If you do that you will be able to "keep in step with the Spirit", and do your part in creating a healthy youth ministry.

*Since we live by the Spirit, let us keep in step with the Spirit. Galatians 5:25*

If your Bible Proficiency wasn't adequate, then you could make part of your study time your devotional time. I worked through most of a ministerial training program (those courses that were Bible based) in my devotional times. In fifteen to thirty minutes a day, I completed one course after another, and in less than five years, I was able to complete an approved ministers training program. I have since completed a Masters in Biblical Literature through a seminary extension program. All of these have helped me to continue to grow.

If your Bible proficiency was adequate, you need to do something that sets the scriptures before you daily. We grow daily or die gradually. Each stage of life requires more of you than the previous one. Fortunately, each day's lessons learned prepare you for tomorrow.

Here are some potential avenues you might pursue to keep you growing.

- Read a chronological Bible for your devotions so that you get a sequential view of scripture.
- Take a topic in scripture that you want to learn more on or understand better. There are plenty out there that most of us don't fully understand; heaven, hell, sickness, death, suffering, etc.

- Do your devotions in a second language. It can help you become more proficient in the language as well as get a different slant on the scriptures.
- Read a paraphrase version of the Bible, realizing it is a paraphrase.
- Find some good devotional life books that challenge you personally. Some classics that I can recommend will probably always be available and always present a challenge.
  - *My Utmost for His Highest* by Oswald Chambers
  - *Foxes's Book of Martyrs* by John Foxe
  - *Three Steps Forward Two Steps Back* by Charles Swindoll
  - *The Pursuit of Holiness* and *The Practice of Godliness* by Jerry Bridges
  - *Revivals of Religion* by Charles Finney
  - *Streams in the Desert* by Mrs. Charles E. Cowman
  - *Operation World* by Patrick Johnstone and Joseph Mandryk  This is a prayer guide that enables you to pray for every country in the world and their key spiritual issues.
  - *Painting The Two White Lines* by Mark Schaufler (Christ's Commands in Today's Setting)-Not a classic but I know we have them for you.

Being in the vine is critical for your future fruit. Learn what it takes to keep you in it (John 15). Even though this may seem to minimize the time you have for ministry, it will maximize your impact in the times of ministry you do have.

You will find that you never have enough time. Here are some proven ways to gain time that you can put back into your family, work, ministry, and devotional life.

- Have a place for everything and put it back A.S.A.P...
- Home- Create a filing system that works for all your household issues and USE it.
- Ministry- Create a filing system that works for all your ministry issues and USE it.
- Work- Create a filing system that works for all your work issues and USE it.
- Return your phone calls A.S.A.P. If they called you they are more likely to be there now than if you try later and they will appreciate your thoughtfulness.
- Go through your mail daily and put it all where it belongs; recycle, bills, read later pile, etc.
- Use postcards or letters if people are difficult to reach by phone or e-mail.
- Completely clean your vehicles after each major use.
- Put all things away after each youth event.
- Keep your financial records, church or home, on one page so you know when you have paid the bills. Out of control finances will worry you to death.
- Drink a glass of water each time you're near the kitchen or bathroom
- Don't do what others can or already have done

- Learn how to say "no" so you can say "yes" for what is important
- Read book summaries not entire books
- Plan each day with the understanding that you can't finish many projects quickly. Instead, you will be able to accomplish one segment of a project and then have to wait for someone else to respond, get some more information, etc. before you can move on to the next segment of the process. You have to start well in advance of most big projects.
- Plan each week
- Plan each year
- Don't make decisions without enough information
- Research time eliminates confusion time
- Call around before you shop, don't drive
- Take things to work on when you go to the dentist, get your oil changed, or play chauffeur for your kids.
- Before you drive somewhere, mow the lawn, or are involved in other brainless activity, read something that you can think about.
- Always have a pen and paper handy or your PDA
- Find out when your prime time is and then use that for what matters most. I am a morning person. My best time is then. It also means I can't do too many late nights or I forfeit my best times for getting things done.
- Find a pace that works for you for the long run. Life is not a sprint, it is a marathon race. Exercise, eat right, and rest (remember the Sabbath).

When traveling-

- Listen to books on CD or cassettes and learn.
- Use a dictation recorder for letters, thoughts etc.
- Let others drive and do whatever you need to while they drive.

Finally, avoid the appearance of evil. Do not do anything that would endanger your spiritual future. Keep great financial records of all your student's money and how you spend it. Don't be sloppy in the area of finances.

Don't spend time with the opposite sex that could be questioned. Don't give them rides home unless you have others in the vehicle with you. If you have a group, drop off the opposite sex before you drop off the last student of your gender.

When you counsel make sure it is in a public place in the church or that your door is open or has a window. Whenever possible don't get into counseling relationships with people of the opposite gender. This area has wiped out more than one well-meaning person.

If you have a past of illegal or immoral activities, you need to deal with that, before you get involved in ministering to the youth.

Disciplining yourself in these areas will keep you healthy. Two of the cancers of life, fear and worry, also need to be dealt with so they don't destroy you before your race is done. Your ability to deal with these menaces will enable you to help students who are often crippled at an early age.

*For you did not receive a spirit that makes you a slave again to fear, but you received the Spirit of sonship. And by him we cry, "Abba, Father." Romans 8:15*

Fear comes in many forms. We can miss a free throw at the foul line, avoid a phone call, ignore some physical symptoms, or neglect prayer time because we are ashamed of our actions. Each of these makes us a slave to apathy and inaction.

But we don't have to live that way. Here is a scriptural understanding of fear and what we can do about it when (not if) it strikes.

- F=Forgetting
- E=Every
- A=Available
- R=Resource

The verse in Romans says that we can ask for help in any situation that strikes fear in our hearts. Then we become the servant of all resources instead of the slave of fear. Father God (Abba) has a solution, help, or strength for us in the situation. Going to Him for help will enable us to make the free throw, the phone call, address the symptoms, and go to Him.

As we face our fears, then we can pass the strategy on to others. Students are in a time of constant change. Fear can easily creep in and paralyze them. Equip them to live out their life facing their fears as servants of God not the slaves of the unknown.

*The one who received the seed that fell among the thorns is the man, who hears the word, but the worries of this life and the deceitfulness of wealth choke it, making it unfruitful. Matthew 13:22*

*Who of you by worrying can add a single hour to his life?*
*Matthew 6:27*

In an unfruitful and short-lived life, worry is often the cause of many physical diseases that exist.   There are more symptoms but the roots are what we need to address.

Worry is an early response before full-blown fear takes over.   Instead of allowing worry to run its course, we need to learn how to respond to it by asking some key question.

- Do I need to find out more about this?
- Do I need to do something about this?
- Do I need to pray about it and finalize something with God?

Sometimes God gives us information to get us going long before we would on our own.   If we do not respond with an appropriate action we may worry instead and create the problem He was trying to help us avoid.

His promptings in our lives should become the first steps in action on our parts.   As His servants, we do not know all the dynamics of everything and we need to continue to be responsive servants even though we have titles of leadership.

Promptings can also have other sources.  Our enemy, our past, and our inadequacies can all be the source of the signal that starts worry in us.  Take the time to recognize the source before you consider your response.

*Dear friends, do not believe every spirit, but test the spirits to see whether they are from God, because many false prophets have gone out into the world.  1 John 4:1*

If you need to deal with an issue, then go to Father God in prayer and get the first steps to take. The key is an appropriate action not fearful reaction.

I was a lifeguard for several summers working my way through college. As a part of the training, we learned a definition for panic. Panic-the sudden, unreasoning, and overwhelming fear, in the face of real or fancified danger. Too many people live in panic mode. In that condition they do things that negatively impact a lot of people's futures.

Stay connected to the vine and help be a part of a healthy youth ministry. Do not grow the fatal weeds of fear and worry. We have enough of that crop growing already.

#  Students-What are they Anyway?

There is no such thing as a typical teenager. They are exposed to so many ideas and philosophies that they are like a stew full of the ingredients of their exposure. You must also take into account Father God's original purposes and plans that He has built into their DNA.

You could describe them a thousand different ways, but for planning purposes, you need to take into account at least these nine key categories. It will enable you to plan to hit the targets they represent and see change in their lives. Disciples are the product of calculated opportunities for growth. Hitting your targets facilitates that growth.

Whether you adopt my designations or not isn't the point. The point is, know your students and take them from where they are to where Jesus wants them to be. Utilizing these target descriptions we were able to move our group to healthy growth. This information has also helped the hundreds of youth groups that I have worked with as guest speaker, staff trainer, or consultant.

Understanding your targets will also enable you to deal with the causes and not the symptoms of the actions you see. Treating symptoms doesn't produce permanent change or health. Instead, the temporary change only postpones a bigger problem.

For example, if you have a rowdy bunch of junior high boys you may conclude that they are all in rebellion and hit them hard with a list of rules and consequences. That may quiet them for a time, but that fatal mistake will probably drive them away. If they leave, your high school ministry will have some terminal diseases that will infect the few young men you still have (fatal apathy) and all the young women (looking for their Adam in other pastures) in your care.

If instead you knew that:

- students learn best when they participate in the learning experience
- and that young men thrive on success,

you would restructure your teaching time and work with, not against, what they are. In time, you would have reached them, trained them, and prepared your high school group for health.

Our nine target descriptions are Adams, Eves, Disciples, Deciders, Distracters, Hurt, Healing, Healthy, and the Gifted. Knowing them will allow you to properly minister to the causes instead of the symptoms you see.

# Adam

Adam had purpose and success from the very beginning of his creation (Genesis 2:15-20). He worked in the Garden with God and named all the animals in his spare time. That is a cornerstone of youth ministry to your young Adams-purpose and success.

Unfortunately, they have several things that make this difficult in a typical church setting, if you don't understand their unique needs. First, they mature slower than the Eves. That means that they lose in any kind of competition or comparison setting. Eves often win the volunteer opportunities because they are suited at a much earlier age for verbal challenges. They will usually do a better job and eventually the Adams quit trying.

Their verbal skills are further hindered by the cracking voice syndrome that hits somewhere in the Junior/Senior high school years. They may have developed athletic or computer skills but not the verbal skills.

In a typical church, if Adam is going to be involved, he had better be verbal or musical. At fifteen, that isn't typical of an Adam.

Barry was all sport and no church. His mother made him attend and expected the youth ministry to fix all the years of damage caused by her irresponsible lifestyle. Sitting in another church service wasn't what he needed. Like any Adam, he needed something very different.

Most churches have far more females than males. That's because the female target is easier to hit, so more females attend. Churches tend to cater to them although most of the time they don't realize it.

Proverbs 29:18 KJV says that without a vision the people perish. Few males can see themselves devoting their lives to an activity that only requires you to give lip service, talk, or sing, especially when they can't compete with the girls or ignore their own cracking adolescent voices.

In Acts 8:26-38, we read about the Ethiopian Eunuch and how Philip shared Jesus with him, beginning in Isaiah, where he was reading. Begin with Adam where they are and bring Jesus to them that way.

Barry started to show some interest after a pick up tackle football game at his apartment complex. I was bruised but had met him at his Isaiah. He joined our flag football team and began to hear other young men's testimonies and see their lives. In time, he went on our mission trips and became a part of the drama team, yes, the jock. Today, he's a youth pastor. He saw that it was more than just talk and he realized how he could be a part of this incredible enterprise called the Kingdom of God.

Quite a change from the young man who resisted the thought of church as he had known it  and who came wearing only boxers, slippers, t-shirt and a hat, three hundred and sixty-five days a year.

We were able to utilize the sport world to reach and disciple a lot of Adams. Covered in mud, blood, and soaked in rain, we bonded with each other and Christ. An Adams' halting testimonies at halftime or the high fives after a homerun all became part of their spiritual journey. New lessons were learned in unforgettable ways.

Sports work for some but not all. In my photo collection are several young men in the back of a truck full of firewood. Terry is in that group. He wanted to serve God and felt called to the mission field but didn't seem cut out for it. His grades weren't that good, he flunked Spanish, and his large frame grew faster than his coordination did. But he knew how to work.

That year we cut and sold over forty cords of firewood for a mission project. That earned $1600 in 1989 and impressed everyone who worked on the project, 90% Adams. He found his niche in construction and, after finishing high school, left to be a missionary, building houses in Mexico.

Young men need to have a Godly vision and it is only possible if they have some success in the Godly realm. Why do so many pour so much into sports with morning practices, potentially serious injuries, and great sacrifices? It's because at some point, they had some success in their activity.

When you're five, you can score a goal in soccer just like on TV. When you are eight, you can shoot a basketball that goes through the hoop just like Michael Jordan did. When you're eleven, you can run back a kickoff for a touchdown just like … okay, you get the picture. But what can you do in a typical church setting? Help them find purpose and success in the work of the Church.

Once you have some Adams who have found a place in the church, other Adams can follow in their footsteps. Once we had our first one (Evan), there was a long line of Adams who set the pace for years to follow.

Our culture thrives on competition. Unfortunately, it is a fatal attraction. Competition crushes all but the select few. The cold hard statistics are that only one out of every million men who play basketball in high school will play in the NBA. Each loser, eventually everyone, is cut from the team and then crushed. We have no place for anyone except winners.

Dealing with failure is not a strong point in most young Adams. The first Adam showed us the thread of pride in his life when he blamed Eve for eating the apple. Pride is still an Adam characteristic that will have to be dealt with in our ministry to them. Pride often leads to another area of weakness, anger.

Scripture shows us Jesus getting angry but never crossing the line to sin. Most young Adams do not know how to do that. Instead, they fall into the trap of silence or cataclysmic events that make newspaper headlines.

We see daily examples in the news of another murder-suicide by an Adam who never learned how to deal with his anger. That failure opened the door for the thief and he stole more lives than any heart can bear to lose.

*In your anger do not sin: Do not let the sun go down while you are still angry, and do not give the devil a foothold. Ephesians 4:26-27*

*The thief comes only to steal and kill and destroy; I have come that they may have life, and have it to the full. John 10:10*

Do not let that happen in the Church. Jesus has a place on the team for everyone. If Adams do not find their place in the Kingdom, they will get involved in all kinds of substitutes. Jobs, cars, sports, computers, or Eves may all be the chosen menu item that each culture has to offer.

Adams also struggle in their attempted relationships with Eves. They do not understand them and are too often pressured into these relationships by an Eve or peer influence. Lust then plays into the equation as sexual drives are confused for love or compatibility.

Lust of any kind is a major problem. Lust can be defined as:

- too much,
- too soon,
- too fast,

- too often.

Sex before marriage, overweight students, binge behavior, pornography, and gambling are all indications that people are out of control.

*It is God's will that you should be sanctified: that you should avoid sexual immorality; that each of you should learn to control his own body in a way that is holy and honorable, not in passionate lust like the heathen, who do not know God;*
*1 Thessalonians 4:3-5*

Waffles also help describe an Adam and how he functions (from the book *Men are Like Waffles, Women are Like Spaghetti* by Bill and Pam Farrel). When he's in a waffle grid he is all there. If it is interesting and engaging then it gets his full attention. If it isn't, he can't stand being there.

In his waffle grid, he can also block out the things that are happening in other grids. Men can flourish in a grid even if other grids are going horribly. This is often helpful until it collides with the Eves capacity to think about multiple issues simultaneously (thus the spaghetti description).

Generally speaking, the Church has missed the Adam reality. It is structured in such a way that most Adams can't find the purpose and success they are wired for and so they leave. That is perpetuated as any new male walking into a church will be surrounded by perfume and estrogen. Unless he is looking for a wife this environment won't foster his spiritual growth.

Fewer men in the church mean fewer women can have a believing husband. That spawns all kinds of sexual problems and frustration issues for the Eves. Unbelieving men then raise kids, run businesses, and influence the political machines of the world.

In many countries like Japan, the Dominican Republic, Thailand, etc. an Eve is almost certain to stay an unmarried woman if they become or stay a Christian. For a relationship-based Eve, that is an incredibly difficult thing to ask.

Yes, the Adams need all the relationship information that Eve does. Plan that in, too. But don't neglect the things that are unique to Adam, or they won't hear the relationship material that they also need.

An effective youth ministry must take these factors into account to properly hit the Adam target. If you do you will see a healthy group of young men and give your Eve's a chance at health as well.

# Eve

After some time, God brought Eve into the picture to be a staff for Adam (Genesis 2:21-24). She was created from Adam for relationship with Adam. To this day, her happiness and security is found in successful relationships. She could have cared less if Adam was a ditch digger, president, or gardener; it was the relationship that she lived for, in the context of purpose and success.

That relational beginning has continued to this day, as successful relationships are the key to a healthy Eve. The challenge is that they want and need them before they have the needed tools. It is also usually before we realize that they need them.

I have polled thousands of women, and most agree that the Junior High years, ages 12-14, are the toughest ones in their lives. Every area that has a relationship in it is changing and they do not feel ready to meet the challenges. If they fail in those relationships, their security is drastically impaired, and they shy away from relationships the remainder of their lives..

Their quick physical maturity is not matched by an equally quick relational or verbal maturity. Unfortunately, because they look like they are old enough to handle the situation, they are expected to. This Eve reality is our mandate to equip them for successful relationships in the context of purpose and success.

"How to have relationships" at home, school, work, with young men, Father God, etc. is the theme you must stick to, to see your women grow in their health and life. Some issues can be covered with the Adams around, but many things need to be dealt with only among the Eves.

Failures in past relationships also tend to impact the Eves longer. Their past is much more a part of their present and future than you will find with the typical Adam. Topics like bitterness and forgiveness usually have their root in broken relationships. Thus, women get the descriptive spaghetti illustration to explain their way of life.

On a plate of spaghetti every noodle is connected to every other noodle. That is seen in the thought processes of an Eve and in their emotional health. Every noodle needs to be okay before they are okay.

During a recent ministry to Junior High students, I asked them what their fears were. Here was the list that the Eves gave me. As you will see, they all have to do with how they perceive relationships succeed. Unfortunately, they are trying to make relationships happen with the wrong tools.

- Getting fat
- Relationships
- Appearance
- Boys
- Getting abused
- Lesbians
- Weight
- Being an outcast
- Not looking good
- Rejection

Tanya was all about relationships, at home, school, and with "Adam". When it was over with her Adam, her junior year of high school, she mourned the whole next year as periodically the calendar would bring up another anniversary she and "Adam" had experienced the year before.

There is no such thing as "puppy love" anymore in our culture. Between the easy phone access, internet chats, instant messaging, and their own cars, your dating couples spend more time together than most married people do.

In weeks they can become very bonded, especially if they are sleeping together. With this level of intimacy so quickly, dating is like marriage without the ring. Thus, a break up is like a divorce without the legal paper work.

Too many Eves are involved sexually as a substitute for a real relationship. It's all they have seen their entire lives and they're giving it a try. When I asked one sexually active Eve about her activity, she knew it did not agree with her Christian ethic but she said, "At least for a while I feel loved."

If you're hitting the Adam target, then your Eves have a chance. If you aren't, then your Eves will be looking, sometimes desperately, for an "Adam" somewhere else. Don't be surprised by what she settles for.

In her "Adam" training, make sure you help them establish boundaries. What is appropriate touch, kissing levels, etc. Teens today often consider virginity anything in the sexual area outside of full intercourse. Oral and anal sex, group masturbation, and lesbian activity are sometimes mainstream teen activities. Remember the fact that teen relationships are more intense and happen sooner than ever before.

Relationships that used to take months to develop now take weeks. Physical intimacy that used to be reserved for someone special is dished out to anyone that is dated. Do not assume anything when you help them establish healthy boundaries. Remember what they see in the media and maybe even at home is instant relationships with all the bells and bedroom activity in the first scene.

Help them to understand the Adam world and their distinct difference. If they do, their chances for long term relationships increase.

Your Eves, more than Adams, may be victims of the sexual crimes of abuse and rape. When we discuss the "Hurt" target it will typically have more Eves than Adams.

Dealing with anger is different for an Eve than for Adam. They use their verbal tendencies to talk about it with others. Thus, while the Adams are cataclysmic in their anger Eve is contagious, there is no such thing as one angry Eve. Practically you will see it when there is a relationship breakup in your group. Soon lines are drawn and sides are picked. If an Adam dumps an Eve, then half the Eves hate him, often before he even knows he has done something "wrong", while the other half want him to know they are available.

If anger becomes an issue within the Eve ranks, you can have a Civil War on your hands as the gossip, bitterness, and anger mix to spread a poison among your students. It does not have to happen this way, but without training, it is very likely.

Their substitutes can look just like the Adams, sports, jobs, cars, and the wrong Adam. They may even throw in a baby outside of marriage. But their satisfaction level isn't as high with the substitutes. Unhappy Eves will be most of your suicide attempts, runaways, and counseling time. Hit their targets to avoid these issues whenever possible.

Their need to succeed is there as well. But without successful relationships, accomplishments won't keep them in the church. As Eve's accomplishments grow the Kingdom, remember that they cannot be at the expense of the Adams.

*For we are God's workmanship, created in Christ Jesus to do good works, which God prepared in advance for us to do. Ephesians 2:10*

Eves also struggle with lust as much as any Adam does. As we addressed the wide range of topics that lust includes you will see the need to equip your Eves to address that problem as well.

Eve also has a unique trait that should be addressed. Eve was deceived. This isn't a sign of inferiority but an issue that continues to be a problem today. Deception comes in a variety of forms but your students will need to deal with it in these ways.

"If you love me you'll sleep with me."
"This is a sure way to lose fifteen pounds."
"If I could only look that way I'd be happy."

Each of these areas of deception boils down to security in their relationships. Often if they have a good relationship with their dad, these deception areas can be avoided. Too often dad isn't there and these areas will have to be addressed.

How does the typical church do with most Eves? Okay by accident, not design. Design your ministry to your Eves so that they are healthy when they graduate from your ministry. That will help ensure the future of the church. That should include plenty of time for them to deal with their wounds and their unique challenges of growing up too fast to deal with all that comes their way.

## Distracters

Some of your students "have to be there." They sit with their arms crossed and talk to each other in the back row seats. Some have parents in leadership positions; others come from homes that think religion is good for students. You baby-sit for some families, so you get their students. All these reasons produce the same attitude: arms crossed, back row.

If you can keep them there long enough, some of them will leave the back row and join the disciples, who want to be there. If you adopt a strategy that includes participation in the learning experiences you design, then Distracters have a chance.

Don't assume that only Christians come to your sessions. Instead, give people a regular opportunity to hear the Gospel, respond to it, and then live it. Living for Jesus is an incredible adventure. Let them see it. Truth sets people free. Give them that chance.

There are many reasons why people can be Distracters. Some may be in rebellion. Others have seen hypocrisy in the church and don't want anything to do with it. Here is an example that is true for too many.

A man comes up to Lance Armstrong, American Tour de France Champion who beat cancer to continue racing, with a big open hand and says, "Lance, I want to talk to you about your belief in God." "Well," Armstrong answers, "it's not gonna be a long talk."

"Even when I was looking at death, I never thought there was something waiting at the other end," he says. "I just think, Whoosh. You're gone. And that's it."

"When I was a boy, I'd see people who talked about God at church and then went home and beat their kids." Lance says. You wonder if he's talking about his former stepfather, Terry Armstrong, a devout Christian who, Lance says, beat him with a paddle, *Sports Illustrated December 16, 2002 pages 70-71.*

Others have been hurt like Lance. A teacher's immaturity, words from other students, and things that were misinterpreted can all leave wounds that are reopened every time they come to church.

Some students are there because their parents are going through a mid-life crisis and are finding God. Their parents didn't like the way the first half of life went and are ready for some change. Often their teens aren't. They wonder what is wrong with the lifestyle they have grown up with.

For others their home life is so stressful, blended, and broken, that despite the attempts of their parents to serve God and make their family work, they see the problems and no solutions and blame it on the ineffectiveness of "Christianity."

Academically, some have been brainwashed enough to see Christianity as the crutch of history that has proven its worthlessness by such events as the Crusades, Inquisitions, politics, church power, and molesting priests.

Why would you go to school again on Sunday and just listen to somebody talk about something that doesn't have anything to do with the life they live? A few more are in this camp.

Others have struggled with specific sin issues and do not feel comfortable at church at all. It may be drugs, alcohol, or a pornography addiction.

You can address their issues if you know what they are. Spend some time with your distracters so you can know and hit their specific target.

Jack and his brother Terry had to come. Mom was in a tough marriage and was at church whenever the doors were open with the two boys in tow. It wasn't by their choice and home didn't make Christianity look all that great.

But Jack attended one of our casual small groups that was based on gender and grade. It wasn't a discipleship group, because Jack wasn't a disciple. It was a group of guys doing crazy guy stuff. Once they rolled a HUGE boulder off a mountain and probably destroyed enough timber to build a house.

During one of those relationship-building times, Jack realized he could be a Christian, despite what he saw at home, because of the relationship he had with the group leader and became a disciple almost overnight. Now he helps make disciples as a youth pastor. Terry is a gifted worship leader and has his own band. People, who knew their situation, prayed for them. Know your targets and hit them.

Eli was a junior high distracter and his activity definitely said he didn't want to be there. A wise youth pastor asked him if he could help with the overheads for worship. Eli was soon paying attention so he could do a good job (remember the Garden?) and ultimately made the transition to Disciple.

Don't chase off your future disciples by ignoring, scolding, or making all your events too far off the distracter target. Remember to treat the cause and not the symptoms.

# Deciders

Others will fall into the category of the "not sure why they come" students. They can sit anywhere in the room. They are often quiet and without any friends. You can't determine why they come. They come because God is drawing them. They are just like the others. They need to hear and see the Gospel, get a chance to respond to it, and then be given the tools to live it.

*No one can come to me unless the Father who sent me draws him, and I will raise him up at the last day. John 6:44*

Kyle walked to youth group. He smiled a lot but didn't say much, never more than one sentence at a time. I could tell you the place where he would sit. Worship wasn't his thing, he didn't seem to worship even when given the chance, but he was there for most things.

At a certain point he had heard and seen enough. He wanted to get involved and joined the drama team. In time, he would be on a team that won national awards for their excellence and ministry. Kyle was a decider who decided.

Deciders don't worship, after all they aren't Christians yet. They may be pleasant, helpful, and even interact, but until they decide and become disciples, don't expect them or make them do something that would be hypocritical. Forced worship or prayer is an example. Give them the opportunities but respect their refusal if it comes.

Too quickly we call someone a core kid if they show up all the time and assume they are a disciple. Don't assume. Over the years of leading over one hundred short term mission trips, we have had several involved students give their lives to Christ on the trip. They were good kids, church kids, deciders who finally had enough understanding and information to decide.

I have helped train hundreds of youth staff and providing their students with the opportunity for a decision is something that continues to be difficult for many. "What if I give students an opportunity to accept Christ and no one does?" "What if the other students pressure them into making the decision or not committing their lives to Christ?" All of these things can and will happen. Jesus gave people regular opportunities to follow Him. We must do the same thing.

# Disciples

The Disciples need a higher level of challenge and opportunity than the others. Make sure they get it. Lynn was such a student.

*I tell you the truth, anyone who has faith in me will do what I have been doing. He will do even greater things than these, because I am going to the Father. John 14:12*

She participated in many mission trips, memorized the book of Matthew word perfect, learned to play the piano in less than a year so she could help with worship, helped take the drama team to a whole new level, etc. etc. etc.... because she had opportunities.

As busy as students are, you need to provide significant challenges for them in the course of a year. They are up to the challenge if they are healthy disciples from supportive homes. Without the challenges from the Kingdom of God, they will fill their time with school opportunities, jobs, hobbies, sports, and miss out on what they could have done for the Kingdom. Once they get a taste for Kingdom work, little else compares.

Lawrence had been a great student, basketball player, and overall great guy. He was concerned about his lost friends, bringing them to church, but was more of a good citizen than a disciple, until he went on a mission trip his senior year.

That experience altered his life. As he began his first year at a prestigious private college he started to evaluate what his life would look like. If this was it, college life and the people he was getting to know, he wasn't too excited about it. He was reminded that life had been on the edge and worth living during that week in December on a mission trip.

Lawrence and Lynn are now married, pastoring a church, with future plans of being missionaries. Without opportunities as teens, these kinds of futures won't be chosen.

They need opportunities and tools for success at the highest levels that they can possibly strive for. Their growth and strength will also raise the level of maturity and openness with all the target groups. A student can say something half as well as you do, but it goes twice as far with other students.

Even though you need to equip them with every key teaching of Christ, you need to remember that they start with an element of "doubt" just like the first disciples.

*Then the eleven disciples went to Galilee, to the mountain where Jesus had told them to go. When they saw him, they worshipped him; but some doubted. Then Jesus came to them and said, "All authority in heaven and on earth has been given to me. Therefore go and make disciples of all nations, baptizing them in the name of the Father and of the Son and of the Holy Spirit, and teaching them to obey everything I have commanded you. And surely I am with you always, to the very end of the age. Matthew 28:16-20*

There is a full summary of the key teachings that Christ gave us to teach disciples in the section Training for the Real Race. Make sure that you give students the opportunities to make these a part of their lives, not just a part of their intellect. If you do, then their lives can reflect Christ throughout the realities of life.

*Therefore everyone who hears these words of mine and puts them into practice is like the wise man who built his house on the rock. Matthew 7:24*

# Hurt

You will also have to deal with the battle damage of your society. War, death, divorce, AIDS, incest, rape, abuse, poverty, wealth, neglect, pornography, violence, fear, and the normal damage of just growing up, have crippled many students. A few have come through undamaged, but only a few.

In your planning, you need to take into account the hurt, healing, and the healthy. The hurt were a constant part of Jesus' ministry. If you do well with your first ones, they will be a constant part of the ministry. In the woman at the well, we see a number of the ways people can be wounded, people who will walk through your doors as students and staff.

*When a Samaritan woman came to draw water, Jesus said to her, "Will you give me a drink? (His disciples had gone into town to buy food.) The Samaritan woman said to him, "You are a Jew and I am a Samaritan woman. How can you ask me for a drink? (For Jews do not associate with Samaritans.) Jesus answered her, "If you knew the gift of God and who it is that asks you for a drink, you would have asked him and he would have given you living water." "Sir," the woman said, "you have nothing to draw with and the well is deep. Where can you get this living water? Are you greater than our father Jacob, who gave us this well and drank from it himself, as did also his sons and his flocks and herds? Jesus answered, "Everyone who drinks this water will be thirsty again, but whoever drinks the water I give him will never thirst. Indeed, the water I give will become in him a spring of water welling up to eternal life." The woman said to him, "Sir, give me this water so that I won't get thirsty and have to keep coming here to draw water." He told her, "Go, call your husband and come back." "I have no husband," she replied. Jesus said to her, "You are right when you say you have no husband. The fact is, you have had five husbands, and the man you now have is not your husband. What you have just said is quite true." John 4:7-18*

As a Samaritan she has a heritage wound. Just because she was born into that household and community she is labeled, "a Samaritan." Many of your students have some label or experience that they inherited because of the family they were born into. Those can run very deep.

Rejection is a wound that we can incur at almost any time from almost anyone. Students live in a world where rejection is part of the story as people are cut from teams, parents move, and teachers have to correct the student's work.

God wounds are ones we often overlook *("If you knew the gift of God.")*. Each of us at birth is trying to figure out God. We're so small and He's so big. The way we picture Him and how life really works can produce some big wounds especially when we *"don't know the gift of God."* Why me? Why them? Why this? All of these statements are responses to wounds that people have because they "don't know the gift of God."

The gift is that we can know Father God because of Jesus His son. God doesn't have to be a far away word. It can be as Jesus taught us, a relationship like that of a Father.

When we don't know God or His ways we can be very confused by how life works. We can end up giving Him the blame for the pain of life when it can be better traced to the choices others have made or the realities of change. This is covered fully in another book by the author, *Finish the Race-Know the Coaches.*

Water is necessary for the daily wear and tear that life gives to the human body. Water flushes out toxins and gives you a chance for a healthy tomorrow. Life has a daily wear and tear to it that only the living water that Jesus spoke of can take care of. Without the living water, the toxins aren't flushed out and you carry wounds into tomorrow instead of health.

Spending time with Jesus on a daily basis helps us deal with those daily wounds and keeps their impact to a minimum. Remember the First Aid Kit.

Five husbands used to be hard to imagine, but not anymore. I've spoken with people who can account for eight. The amount of pain that failed relationships bring to the daily issues of life is hard to calculate. It is there and you will have to deal with it.

Avoiding the hurting people will eliminate a large section of youth culture from your ministry as well as eliminating key aspects of your discipleship ministry. No one matures in his or her Christian faith without having to take care of the pain of the wounded.

Here are some of the reasons why so many of your students will fall into the category of hurt or healing.

- 26% of all families with children were headed by a single parent. U.S. Census Bureau 1999
- An estimated 42% of all custodial parents had never married, 38% had divorced, only 5% were widowed. U.S. Census Bureau 1999
- In 1997 340,000 grandmothers were raising their grandchildren without grandfathers or the children's parents present. U.S. Census Bureau 2000
- In 1998, 36% of Hispanic children, 14% of white children, and 64% of black children lived in single parent homes. U.S. Census Bureau-"America's Children: Key National

Indicators of Well-Being, 1999." Forum on Child and Family Statistics, childstats.gov, July 9, 1999

- The median income for single mother households was $18000, for single father households $30000, while the median for married couples with children was $58000. U.S. Census Bureau 1999

- In 1999, 41% of all births were born to premarital parents. U.S. Census Bureau 1999

- Since statistics have been kept, there have always been more abortions and miscarriages than live births. U.S. Teenage Pregnancy Statistics, www.agi-usa.org/pubs/teen_preg_sr_ 0699.html

- An estimated 40% of all children are growing up without fathers in the home. Peter Jennings, "American Agenda", World News Tonight, December 13, 1994.

These statistics lead to the following behavioral observations:

- Boys living in fatherless homes are two to three times more likely to be involved in crime, drop out of school, and get divorced. Girls living in a fatherless home are two to three times more likely to become pregnant teenagers and have their marriages end in divorce. "Heading Toward a Fatherless Society." by Barry Kliff, MSNBC News, March 31, 1999.

- Children of divorce do worse academically, are more prone to delinquency, are more vulnerable to the appeal of substance abuse, are more likely to bear a child out of wedlock, and are less equipped to enter marriage themselves. "Real Women Stay Married," by Susan Orr, Washington Watch, June 2000.

- Almost 70% of young men in prison grew up without fathers in the home. "American Agenda," World News Tonight with Peter Jennings, January 12, 1995.
- Only 5% percent of the single parent family population attend church regularly. The Hidden Mission Field, by Theresa McKenna, Winepress Publishing, 1999.

As a youth pastor, I dealt with over forty suicide attempts, runaways sleeping on our couch, and multiple visits to the local juvenile detention facility because the hurt don't just lie in a corner and get better.

They try to take care of their injuries themselves and this "self-medicating" results in some of the behaviors we call sin. The typical homosexual was deeply hurt by men early in their lives, abandoned, rejected, and verbally abused, and their self-medication is the homosexual behavior we see.

Suicide attempts are often tied to sexual abuse in the past. They have had a horrific, evil, experience that hasn't been explained to them. Where was God? Why me? Where were my parents? That leaves them vulnerable to other evil. They don't feel they can stop going down the path that evil has had them on before. Suicide seems like the only option available to them.

Drug and alcohol use self-medicates anyone to the painless point of avoidance, at least for a while. Unfortunately, they also stop maturing, their chances of successfully dealing with the future go down, and that promotes the constant use of their medication of choice.

Sexual promiscuity enables someone to feel loved, even if only for a moment or a night. Like all self-medications, this one has a very high price tag. Sexual diseases, an inability to maintain relationships, and the scars of a guilty conscience, all conspire to bury someone. Then you add the inevitable abortion, or single parent status, and you have someone who may smile on the outside, but is dying inwardly.

There are three key areas you help them in: trust, level paths, and open wounds.

*Hope deferred makes the heart sick, but a longing fulfilled is a tree of life. Proverbs 13:12*

People that shouldn't have hurt them have hurt these students. Don't add another person to their list; you. The word trust can help you to see what it will take.

- **T** - Time, and it can be a lot of it
- **R** - Reliable and consistent in your actions under all circumstances
- **U** – Understanding, and you prove it by asking them questions, not already knowing what to do
- **S** - Success in this "Jesus option" that they can experience
- **T** - Tested, and you will be, the only death threats I ever received came from hurt students in our youth ministries

*Therefore, strengthen your feeble arms and weak knees. "Make level paths for your feet," so that the lame may not be disabled, but rather healed. Hebrews 12:12-13*

Level Paths are something they need in order to facilitate success and positive experiences with God before they will trust Him with their lives and pain. You can provide those, rather than requiring them to act a certain way because they should. You can do that as you include them in your walk with Christ and the group's progress. You can do some very practical things to help them connect with Father God.

- If you do a fund raiser and they were a part of it, emphasize the positive impact the funds will have on the project. They were a part of that success.
- When you pray with people make sure they get opportunities to be prayed for too. They need to experience God's touch for themselves.
- Take time in your gatherings to pray for current events as a group. Continue to keep them updated when the news show that God's hand helped in the situation.
- In your teaching and preaching times, make sure you show how practical God's word is and how much better of a place the world would be if everyone did it His way.
- Make sure you have opportunities for the hurt students just as much as the spiritual giants.
- Don't compare one student to another in regards to their abilities, instead rejoice with those who rejoice and mourn with those who mourn.

Open wounds are an opportunity for you and others to put your first aid kits to use on others. (Remember Matthew 5:43-48 & 6:14-15)

Evan came with a friend one Sunday morning and did not leave until he was done with high school. He came from a home where mom lived with a guy as he and his two siblings did the best that they could with mom's current choice. He was also dyslexic. That made school almost impossible and sports a challenge, because he couldn't read the play book or rules.

It wasn't too long before he accepted Christ and began his journey from hurting to a healthy young man who was our first strong Adam. He started a Bible study on his high school campus while he would cry through his problems at home. He was healed of his dyslexia, but still had to learn to read better than his current second grade reading level. Every step Evan took left a trail of tears behind. Ultimately, the time came when he was healthy enough that he did not have to cry all the time.

Eventually his whole family came to Christ. Eventually he became healthy, eventually. Often youth ministry is an emergency room that keeps their patients alive after the last crisis. Keep them alive and watch them grow.

Her stepbrother had sexually abused Shelly when she was a darling, curly haired, little girl. She still lived in the same house with her now twice divorced mom. We met when she began to date a young man who attended our group. They became sexually active under his promise of marriage and a great life together. When that fell apart, she did too. She would make over half a dozen serious suicidal attempts before she stabilized and began to take steps towards healing.

During the worst six months, the best we could do was keep her alive and let her see that we, Father God and us, could be trusted. That was over a decade ago. I heard from her mom recently that she had just participated in a mission trip to Croatia. Wow!

In the middle of all that, we could not see a success story. However, the Great Physician has the capacity to help even those with the most serious injuries, rise up and walk again. Read the rest of the story about the woman at the well in John 4:19-43 and be encouraged as you prepare to minister to your hurting.

The steps that a Hurt student will take may seem small but each one is important. We use a simple salvation bracelet on many of our mission trips. It has five colored beads that help share the Gospel story. We have had Hurt students help put thousands of these together. Then when we have ministered with the bracelets they made we get them pictures of the impact and the people wearing them. That is a small step.

When they give in an offering, that is a small step. When they share a testimony; that is a bigger step. When they help paint a widow's home that is a another small step. If they work in the nursery, that is a step. In time, small steps will lead to walking and running.

# Healing

Those that are healing become a part of the team that helps the hurt keep going. Their testimonies, their example, and the attitude changes are essential for the hurt to see. Healing does not happen overnight, and each small step needs to be encouraged.

Bernie was too good looking for his own good. Girls had lined up to date and mate with him before he gave his life to Christ. Nevertheless, this behavior was also a cover up for some significant wounds he had received growing up, the self-medication story.

As a new Christian, some things changed right away but Sundays usually included a confession of his sexual activity earlier in the weekend. When he came with the exciting story that he hadn't slept with anyone that weekend, we rejoiced in the progress. Small steps walk someone slowly away from a lifetime of sinful and destructive patterns.

That is why you need to create a climate for change (the next chapter). It needs to be a safe place where being real is normal. In this place, everyone can check their masks at the door and deal with the real, ugly, war-torn world that we live in.

In this youth "Emergency Room", patience and mercy become some of the key attributes someone will need to enable the "healing" to take their next messy step.

Activities will also take on a new meaning as students begin the healing process. Remember the bracelets that the hurt put together for the mission trips? The healing student can wear one and be ready to share what the colors mean. This increase in responsibility and risk taking will help strengthen them for their next steps.

# Healthy

Healthy students need their own levels of challenge and involvement. The sky is the limit with them. Offer it. Mission trips, mentoring programs, ministry teams, anything significant and worth doing for the Kingdom of God should be considered for your healthy students.

Opportunities with less risk or stress are more suited for the healing and hurt. However, don't under-challenge your healthy students for the sake of the healing or hurt. That is one reason why you have to think of a yearlong strategy instead of a day-to-day one with your students.

In his book, *Keeping Your Teen In Touch With God,* Dr. Laurent did a study of students who left the church when they left high school. Here are the top ten reasons they gave. As you look at each one you will see how they affected the Adams, Eves, Disciples, Deciders, Distracters, Hurt, Healing, Healthy, and Gifted students that walk through your doors. As you look at the list, I think you will see that you can directly influence most of them and eliminate the church exodus.

1) No meaningful role was found in the church (Give them one!)
2) The negative influence of media (Use it to teach the positive truths of Christ's teaching)
3) Poor relationship with parents (Equip both for good relationships)
4) Low self-esteem (Help them find God esteem)
5) Poor relationship with youth pastor/worker (Don't be a jerk!)
6) Negative peer influence (Positive Godly peer influence exists in a healthy youth ministry)

7) Authoritarianism in parents (Equip parents, they are rookies at this part of life)
8) The struggle for emancipation from parents (Often your ministry opportunities for them will provide that)
9) Negative concepts of religion (Let them participate in the real thing)
10) Lack of family harmony (Equip both sides of the problem)

What you do with your students will depend on who they are, where you live, and what gifts you and your staff bring to the ministry table. I am providing you with the ministry opportunities we provided for our students so you can see some of the possibilities, not be intimidated by the list.

- Juvenile prison ministry team-Adams only
- Worship team
- Drama team
- Bible quiz team (remember Lynn who memorized Matthew?)
- Helpers for the church Vacation Bible School
- Team teachers in children's Sunday School
- Football team
- Baseball teams
- Basketball team
- Two local mission trips (Winter and Spring break)
- One work camp (eight hundred miles away where they processed over half a million pounds of fruit for mission projects in a week)

- Two Mexico mission trips (Mexico City for those out of high school and Juarez for those still in high school)
- Feeding program for street people at Thanksgiving and Christmas
- Choir and communion for shut-ins from the older church population
- Visitation group for new people and those who had been absent for a while
- Evangelism teams for street work in our downtown area
- Basic personal evangelism training three to four times a year
- High school campus ministry clubs

These all contributed towards students being involved in a variety of ways based on a variety of gifts and health levels. The healthy tended to gravitate towards the more difficult and risky ones while others found their level path in some of the less demanding opportunities.

Like all youth ministries, you lose some of your best people all the time (it's called graduation), because you are doing all the right things. Your dream team never stays long but they will pave the way for those that would follow behind them.

Involving students in these many opportunities meant I had many staff and we spent a lot of time communicating the opportunities that were there for the students. That communication included personal invitations from leaders and other students as well as all the paper and announcements you can possible do.

From these opportunities came our small groups where we could disciple students on a small group level. Discipleship did not happen in the big meetings, it happened in these small group ministry teams.

## The Gifted

This category exists because of the unique characteristics that these students have. They don't really fit into any one category although they may have part of all eight within them.

I first noticed some of the needs for this group as I did jail visitation. Many of the inmates were "gifted" musically, artistically, and with poems and short stories. Initially it baffled me why they were in there when they had so many gifts.

It turned out; that was the problem. They had so many obvious gifts that no one had ever wanted to correct them or hold them back despite the weaknesses in other areas of their lives. That stunted their development and when they left high school, they didn't have the character traits to support their gift.

In time, the only way they could easily get by, as they had before with their gift, was through crime. Everyone who thought they were doing the teen a favor by letting them "get by" was actually setting them up for failure in the future.

Is it any different in the church? Probably not. Gifted musicians don't need any moral character. As long as they have a gift, we put them up front. There is a growing list of current "Christian" musicians who have not had the character for a solid life yet have ridden their gift to the stage for years.

We need to make sure we don't do them the same disservice that our culture does. Have the same standard for everyone and make sure they get the tools they need to be successful in Christ's path. They must learn how to deal with all the other discipleship and life issues everyone needs to understand. They are a gift to the church. Don't set them up to end up in the gutter of life. It may not be simple because they have been rewarded most of their lives for what came easy. You may need to give them the needed tools to enable them to flourish on the difficult path.

## Summary

In summary, plan well, pray hard, and do what it takes for the group you have. If you don't take the target groups into account then you will find that your group may end up with pregnant girls and all the guys (some will be fathers, too) with "attitudes" in the back of the room. Students that could have been your key students will spend all of their efforts at schools, scout troops, and on the sports teams that abound in the teen world.

First, evaluate what you have in your student pool. You see these students in the course of a typical month.

_____% of male students
_____% of female students
Should add up to 100%

_____% of Disciples
_____% of Distracters
_____% of Deciders
Should add up to 100%

_____% of Healthy students
_____% of Healing students
_____% of Hurt students
Should add up to 100%

Names of the Gifted

   -

   -

- 
- 
- 

If you know your student population you can make plans to help them succeed when they begin to follow Jesus. If you don't know them, take the time to. Here are some ways you can accelerate the pace of getting to know them.

- Hand out anonymous surveys to the students. You can ask any kind of question with these
- Hand out anonymous surveys to the parents. Again, you can ask any kind of question with these
- Visit their homes, fifteen minutes there will tell you a lot. Students are a by-product of their homes
- Create games and watch them play. This often reveals the true character of a student
- Visit them at school during an event
- Visit the schools. Other than home, this is their single biggest influence
- Read the local newspaper, letters to the editor, etc. Find out what the community mindset is
- Read local history, it may still be influencing today

Breaking the student population down like this will also help you to recruit other leaders to the team. Certain people will have a heart for certain kinds of students--match them up. Your leaders need success just as your students do.

This will also help you to understand why you do what you do. Normally we all have a heart for a certain kind of student. Mine were the hurt, distracter, and Adams. I hit that target easily but really had to work hard at the others and was grateful for the other youth staff with the different gifts they had.

We really can impact students from all these groups if we start where they are and help them down a path towards discipleship.

# 4 Creating a Climate for Change

Don't we wish we could open up the heads of our students and just pour it all in?  We cannot, and the sooner we realize that and start cooperating with Father God, the sooner our students will have the opportunity to change.

Don't fall into the trap of the "ZAP service" where one powerful move of God changes everyone in every way, permanently.  That's not Biblical and it isn't easy.  Change means that there will be some level of failure and correction.  It doesn't feel good and it only produces the desired change, "in time," "eventually," "later on," "after awhile," you get it, right?

*No discipline seems pleasant at the time, but painful. Later on, however, it produces a harvest of righteousness and peace for those who have been trained by it. Hebrews 12:11*

Those two factors mean it does not happen naturally. You are forced to create an environment where this unpleasant experience can take place and where it is a positive adventure.

Fighting against this will be the feelings, facts, and faith issues. Our culture has decided that pain, a feeling, is bad and pleasure, another feeling, is good. We have all heard it said, "If it feels good, do it." To a certain degree, we have exchanged right and wrong for good and bad feelings, like in the Star Wars movies, "I have a bad feeling about this."

Pain is the only way you will increase a muscle's size, strength, and power. It is also the only way you learn how to deal with some of the uncomfortable realities of life. Sorrow, not a good feeling, is needed to deal with grief and loss. Anxiety is normal before you face a new and challenging task. It hurts the day after you have done something physical.

If we eliminate all our sources of pain, we won't exercise, face crises, or do anything new. Sounds too much like the USA already doesn't it? In addition, our feelings gauge is broken. "I'm so hungry I will die if I don't get something to eat!" "I'm so angry ... I'm so tired ... I'm so ..." All feelings, and often all wrong.

Students will need to learn that feelings are just preliminary information on an issue, not the final word. We need to train them to respond to facts and to learn how to gather them.

For example, Sarah and Josh are a part of a day hike you have prepared as a mini-retreat. Everyone has a sack lunch, water, paper, pen, and his or her Bible. Carrying their own materials in a daypack, everyone heads two miles up the trail before you begin to assign people their quiet place with Father God.

Fifteen minutes into the hike, many students feel like they are going to die.

Fact:

- New muscles they haven't used before
- Not enough water in their system
- And poor physical health.

Thirty minutes into the hike, many students feel like they want to kill you for hating them so much you would sell them on this idea.

Fact:

- You love them so much that you went to all this work so they could experience a unique time with Father God that was inexpensive.

An hour into it, Josh offers to carry Sarah's pack. Sarah feels like Josh may be the one for her, the father of her children, and her knight in white shining armor.

Fact:

- Josh's dad asked him to watch out for Sarah because their dads are friends.

While Sarah is day dreaming (not feeling the pain anymore) she notices that Josh also takes Charissa's pack as well. She feels betrayed and angry.

Facts:

- Charissa's dad is another of Josh's dad's friends

- By the time they reach the end of their hike and are ready to find their quiet place most of the students are not feeling like they want to be there.
- Not all of their issues are true.

If, their feelings aren't dealt with and understood (facts), this may be a wasted day (as bitterness and anger take root and grow). At this point only Josh still has a good chance of a great day with Father God.

Feelings without facts also lead us into fear and panic. How many of us have turned a noise outside our window into an escaped killer, looking for another victim at night? When it was in fact, a cat looking for a meal in the garbage can? Feelings were intended to prompt us to further investigation not just immediate actions or conclusions

Now, back to the day hike, take two:

If students understand what they are experiencing then they can have a completely different reaction to their day. In this regard, you have to think like a coach; how can you help them succeed. Let us do a "take two" on the event.

Before you begin to hike take some time to explain some of the feelings they may encounter and their true source.

Fifteen minutes into it, most of the students realize that they are in poor physical shape and they need to get out and do something more often, maybe even lose some weight. Thirty minutes into it, they are glad you took the time to arrange all this so they could learn more about themselves and Father God, no matter how uncomfortable things are right now.

As Josh helps Sarah with her pack, she realizes that he has a characteristic that she wants in a husband; in about five years.  As she sees him help Charissa, she notes that as a favorable trait as well.

Once you have arrived at your prayer points you have students who have already learned something from the day and are ready to learn more.  Their faith has a chance to grow because they have learned how to deal with their feelings.

Which of the two scenarios would you prefer?  Give them glasses to see life through the eyes of scripture and you can have the better one.  Leave their eyes blinded by the culture and you will get the first scenario almost every time.  When feelings are properly understood, then you can guide them into the new areas of life that change brings about.

For change to become a part of someone's daily life there is a process that we will call the <u>Loop of Life</u> that must be practiced regularly.  It resembles running around a track, which produces some great muscles and a strong cardiovascular system.  As we run each section of the track, it will give us another opportunity to change.

The Holy Spirit fires the starting gun.  John 16:7-16 shows us that the Holy Spirit will:

- Convict us of our sin,
- Comfort us,
- And guide us.

*But I tell you the truth: It is for your good that I am going away.  Unless I go away, the Counselor will not come to you; but if I go, I will send him to you.  When he comes, he will convict the world of guilt in regard to sin and righteousness and judgment: in regard to sin, because men do not believe in me; in regard to righteousness, because I am going to the Father, where you can see me no longer; and in regard to judgment, because the prince of this world now stands condemned. I have much more to say to you, more than you can now bear. But when he, the Spirit of truth, comes, he will guide you into all truth. He will not speak on his own; he will speak only what he hears, and he will tell you what is yet to come. John 16:7-13*

The challenge is; will we respond or run?  Our culture says that we need to avoid all these, if possible.  We will have to relearn how to react.

His conviction is based on His love for us and the fact that He doesn't want to see us or others hurt by our sin or immature actions.  If we are feeling His conviction, we should respond correctly rather than run or try to blame others.  Taking responsibility for our own action is the first step in change.  Knowing that we are loved and that Jesus has a solution for conviction is necessary to make that first step possible.

When convicted, we only have one course of action that will take care of the guilt we feel.  We have to go to Father God and ask for forgiveness in Jesus' name.  We have to go to the cross.

*If we confess our sins, he is faithful and just and will forgive us our sins and purify us from all unrighteousness. 1 John 1:9*

If we don't go to the cross, we tend to try and conceal the voice of God or ignore it.  Ultimately, we avoid church, worship, or reading the Bible.  Due to guilt, our activities change, and we keep ourselves so busy that we fall asleep from exhaustion at night.

- Do your students avoid their guilt or deal with it quickly?
- Have they created a lifestyle that avoids God or one that includes Him?
- Have they learned how to clean up their messes with God?
- Have they learned how to clean up their messes with people?

Giving them the tools and opportunities to do this are all a part of equipping the saints for the work of the ministry. You must remind them of the guilt-forgiveness fact. Give them the opportunity to experience forgiveness almost every time you meet.

Each time they are forgiven, guided, or comforted, it's like making it down the first straight stretch on the track. Forgiveness is a miracle but the miracle isn't supposed to stop once we are white as snow.

*"Come now, let us reason together," says the Lord. "Though your sins are like scarlet, they shall be as white as snow; though they are red as crimson, they shall be like wool." Isaiah 1:18*

For many people, that is all they know about the Christian life. Sin, forgiveness, and going out and doing it again and … you know the cycle. It is as if you are running the hundred-yard dash for training but your event is the marathon.

Let us look at lying as an example. People lie for many reasons. Whatever the reason, you will not grow as long as you lie. Forgiveness can follow, but we have to get to the root of the problem—the cause.

In this case, it's the fear of facing the consequences of their actions. They need to not lie but face the pain of consequences. How does that happen?

Permanent change only happens when something changes inside us and the two key elements are the head and the heart. We need to spend time with God for that to happen. If we do not, then we will only repeat the cycle of sin and forgiveness for the rest of our life.

Help people design their own personal time for God into their schedule. You can help them by having times like these designed into your retreats, camps, outreaches, and services. Until it becomes a personal discipline for them, you will need to help your students and staff have these experiences in their lives. John 14:6 tells us we have that privilege. We need to utilize it.

*Jesus answered, "I am the way and the truth and the life. No one comes to the Father except through me." John 14:6*

## The Comfort of the Father

Time in God's presence will allow us to deal with the heart issues. Here we can unload our pain, sorrow, wounds, and fears. Here He can replace them with the truth that sets us free from the old patterns that used to determine and dominate our lives.

*Praise be to the God and Father of our Lord Jesus Christ, the Father of compassion and the God of all comfort, who comforts us in all our troubles, so that we can comfort those in any trouble with the comfort we ourselves have received from God. 2 Corinthians 1:3-4*

For example, I may be a quiet person because I have made mistakes in the past when I opened my mouth and people made fun of me. Dealing with that in God's presence will replace that with boldness and strength. Only God's touch can heal that area and replace it with what should have been there all along.

The key again? Do the students and staff have the opportunities on their own or do you need to provide it? Either way it becomes a calendar issue. Train them how to calendar for change. Five minute devotions won't work. These things are issues that take time. Give Him enough time to do something great in a life.

## The Renewing of the Mind

The heart and the head are connected and influence each other. We need to complement a healthy heart with the truth from a renewed mind. For example, if parental rejection is an issue then a scripture like Psalm 27 could help set someone free. It may be more than one scripture but the truth has to be understood or the heart will not work in unison with the head. They will fight each other.

*Do not conform any longer to the pattern of this world, but be transformed by the renewing of your mind. Then you will be able to test and approve what God's will is—his good, pleasing and perfect will. Romans 12:2*

*Though my father and mother forsake me, the Lord will receive me. Psalms 27:10*

Your mind is like a filter that responds to things before your heart gets a chance to be impacted. How your mind deals with the issue will determine what happens in the heart.

Most of us know about a War veteran who has struggled as they try to live life outside of the war zone. Other veterans seem to be doing just fine. Why? The condition of their mind determined their reaction. For some who had never seen blood, or understood that war is a result of man's greed and desires, as evidenced in the Old Testament, this was a nightmare that they haven't awakened from yet. Others saw the same action and atrocities and came out grateful. Grateful that their lives were spared and that God had a plan for them to fulfill here on this earth.

One was shattered and another strengthened. One was guilt ridden; another was forgiven. The setting didn't determine it; the mindset of the individual did. Renewing our minds is necessary to help us deal with the past as well as the future.

If I think that Christians will live a carefree, very unbiblical by the way, life with one blessing after another, I can almost guarantee that my faith in God will be shaken on a regular basis.

If I think along biblical lines, then I can face the real issues of life and meet the challenges. I will only think biblically if I'm exposed to the truth and have the opportunity to memorize and renew my mind. You can have the software but if you don't install it and learn how to work with it, it doesn't do you any good.

The question arises; do students and staff have exposure to the truth, as well as time to memorize and internalize it? If so, then the renewing will be an ongoing process. If not, then they will be doomed to repeat the past.

A comforted heart and a renewed mind are key segments

of the track we are called to run on. Each lap around the loop of life will require some time in each of these sections of the track.

## Jesus as Lord

*"Come, follow me," Jesus said, "and I will make you fishers of men." Mark 1:17*

Mark 1:17 is a simple sentence but is it a practiced truth? Is He our coach or is He just an advisor? Are we playing life by His rules or making up our own as we go along. He cannot bless our mess unless it is an honest effort at His plan.

Presenting the Gospel plan of repentance and following Christ is always a part of our work. How often do we do it? Do we present the full claims of Christ or only parts? Do we give people the tools they need to live that life or only frustrate themselves? Are we giving them opportunities to be involved in the activities that Jesus called us to do? All of these have to do with someone giving their lives to Jesus. As their spiritual caretakers, we must give them the tools and opportunities to grow in all areas.

It is easy for Jesus to be Savior. What a thrill to be forgiven, no matter how many times it happens. However, submitting to Jesus as Lord is not usually as easy.

Most of us have some negative experiences with people in authority somewhere in our past. Mine came at the hands of a Little League coach. He had played semi-pro baseball as a pitcher and as a result, he wanted to pitch our batting practice. Unfortunately, he would pitch to us as if he was still in the majors trying to prove he had "the stuff." All of us would have quit if our parents allowed.

In contrast, Jesus is a coach who understands people

more than any person does. I took numerous P.E. classes in college to keep my grades high enough to be eligible for water polo, my sport. I took beginning diving, as well as beginning swimming and other beginning water sports classes, in order to get a guaranteed "A" and help my GPA.

In our first day of beginning diving class the instructor said, "If you will learn to trust me, I can teach you any dive that can be done". At that point, he had his assistant do a simple back dive off the three-meter board. We were impressed, but we were still expecting to get near the edge of the pool and drop in cautiously.

Instead, he instructed us to line up at the high dive to copy the assistant's example. People looked at each other in disbelief; some left the class, never to return. The rest of us took our first step toward trusting him.

He was right. If you trusted him and listened to his individual instruction you could learn to do any dive you had the guts to try. Standing next to the edge of the pool, his instructions always gave you what you needed at exactly the right time. Beginning diving had no limits. Neither does your life, if Jesus is your coach.

If you trust and submit to Jesus, that brings you down to the final stretch of the track with the finish line in sight. Fortunately, the Holy Spirit gives us what we need to finish well.

## The Holy Spirit as the Power Source

Now we're in the regular world with a renewed mind and a life submitted to Jesus. Are we ready to embrace the power that the Holy Spirit has made available to us?

He convicted us before and is wasn't fun. Now He will guide and empower us, if we'll let Him. That means enough prayer time that we pray in the Spirit. That means having a lifestyle that is slow enough, where we can keep in step with the Spirit.

> *Since we live by the Spirit, let us keep in step with the Spirit. Galatians 5:25*

All of these factors will become a part of our lives if we also embrace the painful times of conviction and comfort. We cannot shake His hand and keep Him at a distance when He convicts but give Him a big hug because He gives us power. We need to embrace Him at all times, in all settings, and for all that He does in our lives.

Only a renewed mind realizes that conviction is from Father God and that it is for our good and is based on His love. If that is understood, then we can embrace the power of the Holy Spirit when it is needed. If not, we will never have power for any length of time.

Again, are our people growing in this area and are we giving them the tools to grow? Remember the teacher hasn't taught until the learner has learned. You will recognize that some of your students' and staff's problems are based on one or more of the six key areas covered in the loop of life.

Your distracters are only living in conviction. No wonder they don't want to be there. Your new Christians may be very frustrated and constantly on the verge of giving up. They need some real comfort and renewing times to make it.

Your solid students can become a little flaky if they have hit a lordship issue, something He wants them to do that they don't want to do. Everything was cool with God until He asked me to be a "...". Then the problems begin. For others, they have great zeal but not enough knowledge or power to pull it off.

It can sound complex but at least it can be understood Truth always sets you free, even if it is a long road to total freedom.

With each lap that you take around this track, you become more like Christ. Jesus was with His disciples for more than three years, almost every day, almost all the time. You only have hours with your students. If you can teach them how to run the track by themselves, you will have done them a lifetime favor.

Christians want to run this race, but don't know how. A student's first time around may be with you. When Jesus had His disciples, He accomplished this growth in them through their involvement with Him. More was "caught" by them than formally "taught" by Him.

Your students need to be involved in meaningful parts of the Kingdom (Remember Dr. Laurent's list and the number one need for students, a "Meaningful Place in the Church").

## Jesus and Peter

We also need to continue to create a climate where change is normal. You see, change by definition, also means failure. Failure isn't generally tolerated in many places in our culture. It must be celebrated in the church.

How all this takes place is seen in the relationship between Jesus and Peter. In it are some key principles that we must integrate into the very fiber of all we do with students and staff.

In Matthew 14:22-33, Jesus has spent the evening praying while the disciples head out on their boat. As Jesus approaches them walking on the water Peter is challenged to come out on the water and join Jesus. He does. He was doing something no other disciple had done, until fear overwhelms him and he begins to sink. He began his journey in faith by obeying Jesus and ended it as fear overcame him when he saw the wind and the waves and began to sink.

Our key lessons from this incredible adventure are this:

- Fear and faith always fight
- Jesus reached down to help Peter
- Jesus corrected Peter with the truth he needed for change
- Peter was still on the team.

Halloween is the second biggest holiday in the United States. Our culture is motivated by fear and finds an outlet for that fear in this holiday. Your students and staff will be crippled by fear unless you have a climate where they can step out of the boat and get the help they need.

Evangelism is a key example. Fear stops most people. As you equip them and give them opportunities, make sure you encourage and correct, as needed, those who do get out of the boat. This will produce disciples that set the pace in every area of life.

Next we see Peter and another area we must all grow in; hearing God's voice (Matthew 16:13-28). Jesus has asked who do the people say He is. Several disciples offer opinions. However, when asked, "Who do you say that I am," Peter responds.

If Peter had felt crushed from his water-walking failure, he would not have answered this question. Instead, Christ has created a climate where the disciples can be wrong and in the end learn to be right. Peter gives the right answer. Now Jesus tells him that he has heard from God. Yes, Peter did hear and so can we. Whenever possible, we need to confirm to our students and staff when they are hearing from God.

*Jesus replied, "Blessed are you, Simon son of Jonah, for this was not revealed to you by man, but by my Father in heaven. Matthew 16:17*

After this encouragement, Jesus heaps praise and responsibility on Peter. Nevertheless, doing it right also means we have the capacity to do it wrong.

*"Get behind me Satan! You are a stumbling block to me; you do not have in mind the things of God, but the things of men." Matthew 16:23*

Peter assumed he could answer any question with the wisdom of God. He was wrong and Jesus told him why he was wrong.

What can we learn to help us on our climate control?

- Encourage students and staff when they are right
- Correct when they are wrong
- Do not take away what they have already received
- Hearing God's voice is a process we all need to learn

Finally we see a third key example that we must be able to bring into our ministry community, forgiveness (Mark 14:66-72 & Acts 2:14-41).

Peter had followed Jesus into the courtyard. Inside, Jesus is going through a mock trial while outside Peter is going through a trial of his own. Three times, people question him about his connection with Jesus. Each time he denies that connection.

*Immediately the rooster crowed the second time. Then Peter remembered the word Jesus had spoken to him: "Before the rooster crows twice you will disown me three times." And he broke down and wept. Mark 14:72*

He wept because Jesus had told him he would do this. He also wept because he had heard Jesus say this as well.

*But he who disowns me before men will be disowned before the angels of God. Luke 12:9*

As far as Peter knew, he had just blown his chance with God. Nevertheless, somewhere between then and the day of Pentecost, Peter was forgiven. How do we know this? Peter is the preacher who, at Pentecost, shows that he has learned all three of the key lessons we have stated.

*Peter replied, "Repent and be baptized, every one of you, in the name of Jesus Christ for the forgiveness of your sins." Acts 2:38*

This was a large, hostile crowd, and it was Peter who stood up and delivered the first message that would see a large number converted to the newly formed church. Why Peter? Who else had learned the key lessons.

Peter had already gotten out of the boat before and sank. This time he didn't sink, he knew whose hand to hold. He had already heard the voice of Father God and knew this was God's voice again.  Moreover, he offered the forgiveness that he had already received.

While I was in college, I took a class, which was very difficult for me, "Organic Chemistry."  It required memorizing huge amounts of information.  You could flunk almost all the tests, up until the final, and still get an "A," because it was your final test that showed what you had learned.

It would appear to us that Peter had flunked some big tests and that Jesus was just letting him hang around because He felt sorry for him.  No!  Peter had learned the keys from each of these tough lessons and was using them to open the doors to the future of the church.

If you have that kind of climate, you will give keys to the students and staff to open the future for the churches they will be a part of.  That kind of climate will prepare them for the real track of life that they will run on until the day they die.

#  Training for the Real Race

Too often youth ministry is known as a fun and games approach to childcare in the teenage world. Unfortunately, it has sometimes been true.

You can have fun and use games but they can't be your trademark, only your tools. Matthew 28:16-20 and Acts 1:8 give us the border for the puzzle called youth ministry. It describes the track we are to run on with our lives. It is in one shape or form the race marked out for each of us.

*Then the eleven disciples went to Galilee, to the mountain where Jesus had told them to go. When they saw him, the worshipped him; but some doubted. Then Jesus came to them and said, "All authority in heaven and on earth has been given to me. Therefore go and make disciples of all nations, baptizing them in the name of the Father and of the Son and of the Holy Spirit, and teaching them to obey everything I have commanded*

*you. And surely I am with you always, to the very end of the age.
Matthew 28:16-20*

*But you will receive power when the Holy Spirit comes on
you; and you will be my witnesses in Jerusalem, and in all Judea
and Samaria, and to the ends of the earth. Acts 1:8*

Here are some of the keys we need to get into the very
fiber of our being as we follow Christ and impact students.

- Disciples start with doubt, only experience will eliminate
  it. Remember Peter!
- We must "go" at regular points for some length of time.
- We are called to change nations by making disciples
  which includes teaching them everything Christ has
  commanded us.
- He will be with us as we do this.
- Jerusalem, Judea, Samaria, and the ends of the Earth
  evangelism (Acts 1:8) are the pipe that Discipleship flows
  through.   You cannot have comprehensive discipleship
  without challenging evangelism.

You can use fun and games if they facilitate learning or
living out one of Christ's commands.  The key is that whatever
you do, for and with students, consider these factors.  You need
to create opportunities for them learn to live the life Jesus has
called us to.

If you do not, then everything Jesus said doesn't make
sense and we have misrepresented the Gospel to them.  If we do,
then the disciples will really become disciples.  Deciders will

have the best chance of making the right choice. Distracters will have no excuses.

If you do, then the healthy will become strong, the healing healthy, and the hurt will be on the path to health. Adam will find his place in the garden and Eve will become all that she was created to be as well.

As a youth worker, you don't have time to waste in any other pursuit. Now you can have a creative blast doing it as Jesus did (in Luke 10:1-24 Jesus sends out the seventy-two in two's). You can do it with media or you can do it without. You can do it with money or you can do it without.

It is work but it is well worth it. You can do it with the gift of the pastor/shepherd or without it. It can be accomplished in as many ways as there are people who do it if you do it within the biblical framework based on biblical principles.

Here is a checklist of the key teachings that Christ left for us to use to make disciples. The full text for each command is found in *Painting the Two White Lines*, another book by the author.

Rules of the Track
- Mercy-Romans 6:23, not dead yet
- Grace-1 Corinthians 15:9-10, Paul's secret
- Faith-Hebrews 11 & Romans 10:17 balance

Loving God-Matthew 22:37
- Listen-Luke 8:8, use those ears
- Trouble and fear-John 14:27, peace in it all
- Take my yoke-Matthew 11:28-30, partners in life
- His seed, His harvest-Luke 19:9-10, seeking the lost

- Caught in the act-Matthew 24:45-51, doing good
- Prayer-Matthew 6:5-15, when you pray
- Fasting-Matthew 6:16-18, when you fast
- Giving-Matthew 6:1-4, when you give
- Worship-John 4:21-24, how you worship
- Temptation-James 1:13-15 & Matthew 26:39-41
- Only Jesus-John 14:6, the door is one person wide
- Open for business-Matthew 5:16, lights on?

Loving People
- Love your neighbor-Matthew 22:38-40
- The dangers of love-1 John 2:15, other loves
- Love not lust-Matthew 5:2, don't look or touch
- Love lost, divorce-Matthew 19:3-9, hard hearts
- Love your enemies-Luke 6:27-36, really!
- Anger-Matthew 5:21-23, the thin ice of anger
- Stranger evangelism-Matthew 5:47, your name was?
- Judge "not"-Luke 6:37-38, we are always wrong
- Living without a plank-Luke 6:42, clear vision
- Flunking-Matthew 18:21-22, forgive, forgive
- People versus possessions-Luke 6:31-32, stuff.
- People versus positions-Mark 10:41-45, you're first
- Doing something-Matthew 5:23-26, reconcile
- When things don't change-Matthew 5:11-12, leaving
- The heart monitor-Matthew 12:33-37, your words
- Mission field or missionary-Luke 6:24-26, your actions

Ministry

- Follow me-John 21:22, following Jesus
- The message-Matthew 4:17, repent
- The pace-Mark 10:13-14, love children
- Clothed with power-Luke 24:49, wired with God
- Get ready-Luke 12:47, living ready
- Go!-Matthew 10:7-8, freely give
- Greater things-John 14:12, more than Jesus
- Guess who's coming to dinner-Luke 14:12-14, the poor
- Made for miracles-Matthew 14:15-21, major needs
- Rest-Mark 6:31, even superman sleeps
- Listen-Revelation 3:19-22, he speaks
- Bottom of the ninth-Luke 5:1-8, fish till you're dead
- Saying "yes" when you want "no"-Matthew 26:37-41
- Do not be afraid-Mark 6:47-50, it's Jesus
- Lazarus-John 11:43-44, raising the dead
- Deaf and mute spirit-Mark 9:25-27, know the source
- Not just a headache-Matthew 12:43-45, know the cause
- Healed-Matthew 8:1-3, now what?
- Home town obstacles-Luke 4:23-24, you?
- Evangelism seekers-Mark 10:17-22, when they ask you
- Evangelism seek them-Luke 5:27-28, follow me
- Mercy ministry-Mark 8:1-8, feed them
- Unity-John 17:20-21, one big happy family
- Religion-Luke 11:42, rules and regulations
- The Sabbath-Mark 3:1-6, Jesus' day
- Forgiveness-Luke 5:17-24, ugliest sin forgiven

- Doubting-John 20:24-27, Thomas figured it out!
- If they hate you-John 15:18-19, they hated him first
- Tough times ahead-Matthew 24:9-14, wars and death
- Quitting time-Matthew 24:45-46, until you die
- Baptize and teach-Matthew 28:19-20, the world

To utilize evangelism you need to understand the key basic principles. First, evangelism is a process that involves planting, watering, and harvest.

*What, after all, is Apollos? And what is Paul? Only servants, through whom you came to believe—as the Lord has assigned to each his task. I planted the seed, Apollos watered it, but God made it grow. So neither he who plants nor he who waters is anything, but only God, who makes things grow. The man who plants and the man who waters have one purpose, and each will be rewarded according to his labor. For we are God's fellow workers; you are God's field, God's building.*
*1 Corinthians 3:5-9*

There is planting (getting the seed out, God's Word) and there is watering (prayer and acts of love). Each is to be rewarded for doing it by celebrating obedience not just results. In the course of time, you will get to participate in a harvest too!

Christians want to be involved in evangelism. They want to see their friends and family members come to Christ. But they don't know how unless you equip them with tools and opportunities.

As you create evangelistic opportunities for them you will also have created a framework to disciple them. Evangelism and discipleship need each other to exist. Without the discipline of discipleship, most people don't participate in evangelism. Without evangelism, you can't learn everything that Jesus left for us to disciple and teach (Matthew 28:16-20).

Let's say you decide to involve your students in evangelism/discipleship through a day on your local transit buses. As they gather at 9:00 am, you take an hour to train them in sharing their testimonies and the use of several good tracts. With their sack lunch and ticket money in hand, send them out in threes with a rendezvous point for noon.

As you gather at the lunch rendezvous, you can debrief them on their progress and experiences. Praise those who have been able to do something despite their results-remember the planting and water reality. Set out for the remainder of the time with a rendezvous back at the church at 5pm. At the church, debrief and celebrate the fact that there are now people who have heard the Gospel through this group. Pray for the seed planted and get ready for requests to do it again.

This activity will give you the chance to work on several relationship issues, those that are brought up in their work and among each other, and evangelism questions. There will be more teachable moments in that day than you could arrange in a dozen preaching and teaching times. An event like this would give you a specific target, too. Your healthy disciples would be those most likely to attend.

You can hit your disciples that aren't as healthy another way. Pick another daytime event where you hang door hangers on several thousand homes in your area, obviously a smaller town would be hundreds. With these, you can announce a future event for the church or just get the gospel out through tracts or testimonies from people in your church.

Train them before they go out so they don't step on people's flowers and know how to deal with dogs. By doing many doors you can complete an impressive outreach and increase the chance of something great happening.

While canvassing about five thousand doors, with a group of fifteen and in ten hours, we had one of those "something great" things happen. As one of the doors was approached, the student found an earring on the ground. They put it in the bag along with the information for the church we were helping. This is another great way to involve students for a weekend; do it for someone else a distance away.

Within hours, the church got a call from a very grateful woman. That earring was all she had to remember her recently deceased mother and she had lost it. Her joy was also accompanied by a visit to the church. As our team heard that, they were astounded at how big of a blessing they had been.

As the end of the school year approached, we made it our goal to share Christ with every senior who would graduate from one of our local high schools. We succeeded as we got the name of every senior by looking at the previous year's annual and mailed them a gospel of Mark along with the personal testimonies of several of the students in the youth ministry.

Involving students in these kinds of ways opens their eyes to a variety of key truths.

- There is more than one way to skin a cat;  do evangelism
- You can accomplish seemingly impossible tasks if you get a plan, work the plan, and make adjustments
- Each person's gift can play a significant role in evangelism if you are cooperating with the process of evangelism and not just counting the results
- Evangelism is a team sport.

When you use the real world for training, you always get a deeper impact than you can if you only stick to simulations, classroom, and church events. John 14:12 tells us that we will be doing some great things in our lives. Make sure you expose your students to them while they are within the reach of your ministry.

*I tell you the truth, anyone who has faith in me will do what I have been doing. He will do even greater things than these, because I am going to the Father. John 14:12*

As you work out Christ's commands with your students, you will find endless opportunities to make the Bible come alive to them. By training on the real track, you will see real results in your students. Remember that discipleship is the goal not efficient, smooth, on time, tidy, or sterile.

Putting any of Christ's commands into practice will always work through at least four stages. First the student will need to be exposed to the teaching. With that exposure should come the opportunity to try and understand it.

Then they will begin to experiment with the teaching they have been exposed to. This will show you and them just how much of it they understand and how difficult it may be. Remember this phase may not be pretty as they "try" to make it a part of their lives.

Once they have experimented enough to see how it works they will begin to gather their experience on the topic. In time that will produce a certain level of expertise. If the topic is in an area of their gifting they may be very good at it. For those without the gifting they will still be able to pass their experience on to others.

This process takes time. Your disciples will grow more if they understand and have put into practice five of Christ's teachings than if they can quote fifty of them. Plan this into your efforts with them.

# 6 Assistant Coaches and Trainers

Your scripturally given goal is to make disciples of students. That requires that they first become followers of Christ and then mature enough to sustain that lifestyle in the varied situations that life holds. They must exchange their culture for Christ's commands.

This exchange is not an overnight process. Peter, James, John, and the rest of the disciples had over three years of time with Jesus before He left. That was three and a half years where they spent twenty-four hours a day together. You need to make sure that your training enables them to read and pray effectively on their own.

You can give them a course of study. You can give them things to pray about. However, you must equip them, or someone else must, so that they're growing on a daily basis and not just while they are under your teaching.

Realistically you can only care for about four students. As a part of your planning and training you need to invest in others who will also work with these students. Without them, you will be limited in your impact on students.

As you work your way through this manual you will see that this is much more than a one-person job. Good! This will force you to begin to pray for people to work with you and to let their gifts add to what can be done and how well they are done. Jesus and Paul always had a crew with them.

Do not think you will be the first successful lone ranger in the Kingdom of God. If you insist on that, you will join the other lone rangers that are buried up on Boot Hill. People, who thought they could do it without anyone else, found out that isn't what Jesus called us to do.

It also takes a team to properly disciple people. My gifts are not the only ones in the body of Christ. As people are exposed to all the gifts, they can grow into all that God has for them. If they only see a portion of those gifts, they will miss part of the strengths that the body of Christ has.

Discipleship requires relationships. The more relationships that someone can have with the variety of gifts that are out there, the more maturity someone has a chance of attaining. There are a number of gifting tests (for example, www.teamministry.com) that can help you begin to discover your gifts, which also allow you to see the strengths and weaknesses that you possess. As a result, you can see whom you need to include on your team and how to best utilize them.

Establishing your team will take time, so don't plan too big, too soon. In most youth ministry settings you have to establish yourself and gain the trust of the church people before you get a big influx of leaders and staff. It usually takes about two years for that to happen. It can take longer if you make some big mistakes in those two years or a shorter amount of time if you do a good job of communicating. People can see what they would be doing and how well it is being done by the information you give them.

Once you start to gather a team, take the time to develop them as a team and as individuals. The time you invest in them is not wasted. How big your team is depends on how many potential students you have the privilege of working with.

Jesus worked closely with three and had another nine who were in on most of the action. To determine how many staff you will need, take the youth population that you are trying to minister to and divide that by four. If you get a number larger than one then you need help and just how much help you need. You won't be able to do more than four yourself. That will leave you some time to disciple the staff that end up coming your way.

Generally, you should schedule your time with about half of it going toward students and the other half toward your staff. Now you can guesstimate your "staff quota."

For the sake of illustration, let's assume that you are going to try and disciple one hundred young people between the ages of twelve and twenty-five. That would require 25 leaders. You may only have thirty young people right now but if you don't look ahead you will always be looking around for more leaders when you can't find them.

You may also want to add to that number based on the kinds of students you are reaching. If you have a captive audience of church kids wanting to serve God then this number is sufficient. If you have church kids that are rebellious or just plain lost, you will need some additional help to pursue them. If your youth ministry population is full of students from outside the church then you will need to add some additional staff as well. Knowing your nine different target groups will help you as you break down the opportunities for your staff. Some students don't have the support from home that helps to reinforce what you are doing. They will require more help from your team. Now that you are intimidated by the number of team players you need, you are in the right place.

Assembling this team will require that you get a building permit. For that to happen, two things must be in place: you need a plan that has places in it for volunteers to fill. They cannot do what you do so they need bite-sized pieces of ministry that will take into account their gifts and the needs of the plan. Then you need to pay the price for the permit. You must pray.

*Then he said to his disciples, 'The harvest is plentiful but the workers are few. Ask the Lord of the harvest, therefore, to send out workers into his harvest field Matthew 9:37-38*

Every step of progress in this endeavor will require both a plan and prayer. Get good at getting permits.

As a part of the plan I am including a list of potential places you could use staff as you disciple these young people. Some of these positions are skilled and some are not. Some of your volunteers will be skilled and some will not. Create a plan that has places for any kind of qualified people. You can give them the skill if they stick around long enough in an unskilled task.

Junior High Department dream list of "Your Street, Community Church"

- Secretary
- Assistant
- Intern

- Runaway house
- Sunday school class for guys
- Sunday school class for girls
- Parenting class teacher
- Crisis counselor
- Mid-week service coordinator
- Missions coordinator
- Event decorations coordinator
- Event food coordinator
- Family counselor
- Drama coach
- Worship team coach
- Bible quiz coach
- Publications director
- Web page coordinator
- E-mail specialist
- Prayer coordinator
- Conference coordinator
- Set up and tear down coordinator
- Evangelism coordinator
- Assimilation coordinator
- T-shirt specialist
- Video historian
- Video production coordinator
- Choir coordinator
- Fund raising coordinator
- Camp coordinator

- Teaching substitutes
- Sports ministry coordinator
- Event driver coordinator
- Vehicle maintenance and purchase coordinator
- Purchasing agent
- Phone tree coordinator
- Newsletter coordinator
- Mailing coordinator
- Crisis coordinator
- Small group trainer
- Small group coordinator

Senior High Department-dream list "Your Street, Community Church"

- All of the above plus
- Career guidance counselor
- Pre-marriage counselor
- Financial counselor
- Travel agent
- Senior survival teacher

College and Career Age-dream list "Your Street, Community Church"

- All of the above plus
- Internship program coordinator
- Missionaries in training program coordinator

- Tent makers school coordinator
- Credited college program coordinator
- Wedding coordinator

If my math is correct, we just created over one hundred and thirty-seven jobs. Some of them will require more than one person, so you have a place for just about anyone who has a heart for young people.

To begin the integration process you need to establish a plan. This will help you pick the right people for the right place(s) in the youth ministry plan. We used this plan to integrate more than three dozen successful youth staff. You can modify it to meet your needs in a dozen ways.

First, as people begin to seriously show an interest have a form ready for them to fill out that includes their permission for you to do a background check with the police. There is an example in the Appendix. Perverts and predators of every kind have often had happy hunting grounds in churches. Don't let them near the people in your care. Not only do you protect your young people, you will also protect your legal liability. Make sure you check the references on everyone, no matter how "good" they seem to be.

Now you are ready to enter into the equipping process. These people are now a part of the plan God has given you. As you can see from the number of options people will have to pick from, you need to give them some time to pick an age group, task, as well as the option of gracefully bowing out.

Too often, people volunteer with good intentions but don't realistically have the time or call to be effective. Give them the opportunity to determine that without any embarrassment or pain.

# The Enlistment Path

**Intern**  A person seeking a role in the youth department will spend two to three months in the intern phase.  It takes about two years to become effective in youth ministry.  Therefore, everyone needs to take a good hard look at it before they commit to it.  This time will allow them to hear from God in the process.

Interns attend the weekly Sunday school, mid-week meeting, and leader's meetings.  They will also be required to attend at least one extra event a month.  There is an open door policy with you during this time so that questions and issues can be discussed.  Before they complete their internship, they should have experienced all the age groups at their best and worst.  Small tasks will be given to the intern as they near the end of their time.  This helps them to see where they might best fit in the ministry.  At an agreed upon time, the intern will meet with you and discuss their experience.

Now they can make a knowledgeable decision.  They can commit to training and working with the youth or bow out gracefully and seek another area for their service.  If they choose to pursue youth ministry,, be ready for them.  Now it's time to act.

**Apprentice**  When a commitment is made, the training begins.  A person's personal relationship with our Lord will be developed.  All ministry comes from relationship and a training schedule will be arranged to enable that person to fulfill the ministry role they are now involved in.

On the job training will be supplemented as needed by seminars, meetings, and correspondence courses.  This phase may take months or years depending on the level they are training for and their maturity when they start.

**Leader/Teacher** After training has been completed an individual is now ready for the full daily responsibilities of the ministry they have been involved in. They will meet weekly with their **Administrator/Trainer** and work on improving their skills. In addition, they will learn how to train others to help them. Your goal is to establish them in the ministry so that they are capable of generating genuine ministry and sustaining it on their own.

**Administrator/Trainer** These people are now experienced in an area of youth ministry. Their role can include training, administrating, and nurturing those in their ministry area. As they help others mature to this level, they will be ready for youth ministry in any setting to which God might call them. They will meet weekly with others like them, those they are training, and you. At this point, you function as their **Administrator/Trainer.**

This is an investment pyramid. Unlike the financial pyramids where you get rich from them, you are here to make them rich from you and your experience. This allows a trained, healthy group of people to be there for the students God entrusts to you.

**Servant Task** These tasks don't require the same level of involvement as the ones we have already mentioned. After training has been completed, these people will be capable of fulfilling the task that they have committed to. This may include bus driving, cooking, prayer, mailings, etc. These people will meet weekly with their **Administrator/Trainer.** Their goal will be to successfully complete their task and learn it well enough to train others.

In time, some of these people will want to be involved at a greater level. When this occurs run them through the same process you did everyone else. They will probably make quicker progress since you already have a relationship with these people. Often their early success in basic areas of ministry will plow the road for a larger future involvement.

In time, you should have dozens of volunteers. Investing in their lives and ministries will be one of your key roles in youth ministry. You will find that these volunteers fall into several categories. Some will be seasonal. They have certain times of the year when they can help. Other will help on specific events from year to year. A few will be steady and capable of being trained for larger areas and levels of responsibility.

Pam loved teenagers and loved to cook. Everyone always appreciated her contribution. In two specific areas, she made our youth ministry student-friendly and effective. Most students came to our Sunday school hungry. They were irritable and their attention span was minimized. Her Sunday morning breakfast buffet not only minimized their irritability and increased their attention span, but turned the sometime- students into regulars. When we would attend large conferences, she was a blessing again. While thousands of other students were trying to get a meal at a "fast food" establishment, we were enjoying a barbeque thanks to Pam and her grills.

Rick had served time in prison. He was a step-dad of one of the students. In time, he became a dedicated leader who ran our prison ministry team. His past experience and love for students enabled him to raise up a ministry team of students that had a major impact on youth correction facilities in our area.

Larry came to Christ in his thirties. It wasn't long before he felt a ministry call to students. His involvement in our training program ultimately established him as the next youth pastor in our church after we moved on to itinerate ministry work.

You will get parents of your students, college students, and a mix of people who are looking for their place in God's Kingdom. Help them find it and invest in all of your volunteers. Don't let anyone who qualifies to help be lost in the shuffle, but don't be stupid either.

If you have a college student who has one year of school left, realize unless God says otherwise, that they will be gone very soon. Don't put them into a position that will create problems when they leave. Longevity is one of the key elements to fruitful youth ministry. It takes time to build real relationships, trust, and deal with the real issues in your volunteers and the students lives.

As a part of this investment, help volunteers to balance their family, finances, vocation, and ministry so that they can prosper while they help you. Often people push ministry to the forefront at the expense of something that should be higher up on their priority list i.e. family, personal walk with God, or sound financial living. Priorities need to be in their proper place or their time with you will be short and sporadic or, worse yet, end with a cataclysmic bang. Don't assume that they will do this for themselves.

## Clearing the Rubble

In Luke 3:3-6, we read about the rubble removal that is necessary in every life to receive all that Jesus has for them. We must make way for that new life. Do not be afraid to address the issues that come up as you begin to invest in people's lives.

*As is written in the book of the words of Isaiah the prophet: A voice of one calling in the desert, 'Prepare the way for the Lord, make straight paths for him. Every valley shall be filled in, every mountain and hill made low. The crooked roads shall become straight, the rough ways smooth. And all mankind will see God's salvation.' Luke 3:3-6*

Issues will be found in some of the best intentioned and well-mannered people. Despite outward maturity, these issues destroy people and their ministries if they aren't dealt with properly. Finances, pornography, lust, lying, unforgiveness, bitterness, smoking, laziness, and poor people skills are all things that will surface.

Take time to individually invest in people concerning these areas. If they are trying to move forward, they usually want to deal with them but don't know how. Your job is to help them to deal with the issues and move on.

*Brothers, if someone is caught in a sin, you who are spiritual should restore him gently. But watch yourself, or you also may be tempted. Carry each other's burdens, and in this way you will fulfill the law of Christ. Galatians 6:1-2*

Fear is an area that is part of almost anyone's life. In fact, if you can help people overcome fear, you will dramatically increase your chances of getting enough leaders. Fear usually falls into the following categories in youth ministry.

- They don't know what to say
- Don't know how to say it
- Anger issues

- Afraid of their past
- Not an up-front person
- Unresolved personal issues
- Don't know how to handle crisis
- Have a bizarre work schedule
- Don't know how they could help.

As you can see, we have dealt with a few of these already, but let's make sure that we cover as many bases as possible. As you train people, they will see and realize that there are answers to the tough questions that teenagers ask. Have resources that you can get into your leader's hands on tough topics. Success is one of the best cures for fear.

Learning to communicate is also a necessary skill. There are those who are gifted at it and those who work hard at it. You can fit into either category and be effective. Train people on the "how-to" of basic communication and the specifics of the youth culture.

Anger is a common problem. Several good resources are available which help people deal with anger issues and in turn train others to deal with anger as well. As your leaders are helped, they will have fresh insights for the youth that they work with.

As you can see from the worker dream lists, not everyone needs to be an up-front person to help in your youth ministry efforts. As you train staff and they succeed many, in time, will also take on some up-front roles as well. Again, success is one of the best cures for fear and doubt.

The number one personal concern in most people's lives is finances. This cripples many people as their lives are consumed by this topic. Help them. Have answers. Know financial counselors that can train you or counsel people who need the extra help.

Most people avoid a crisis because they don't know what to do. Youth ministry will guarantee you some crisis times. Crisis times can be handled by the grace of God and proper training. You can train people and as they grow they will learn to walk in the grace that God has for every one of us. Without training, most people will not attempt to help. Therefore, train, train, and then work alongside people who do face a crisis and help them grow from it rather than be discouraged.

Bizarre work schedules exist and are increasing all the time. Take flexible schedules into account as people approach you as possible volunteers. As mentioned, you can have seasonal staff, event staff, and people who just help as they can. Keep all your volunteers well informed. Make sure that everyone knows they are on the team. The status of volunteers may change and if you have been faithful to them, then, when they can be totally committed to you, they will be faithful as well. When they have more time, you will get it. One of the best team building books I've read so far is *Teach your Team to Fish* by Laurie Beth Jones (Three River Press 2002).

## Follow a Plan

Ephesians 4:11-16 sets a model for training that we need to keep in mind. As you read it, you will find that our growth is dependent upon our participation. As a part of what you do, give your people opportunities to do new things. New opportunities enable them to grow.

*It was he who gave some to be apostles, some to be prophets, some to be evangelists, and some to be pastors and teachers, to prepare God's people for works of service, so that the body of Christ may be built up until we all reach unity in the faith and in the knowledge of the Son of God and become mature, attaining to the whole measure of the fullness of Christ. Then we will no longer be infants, tossed back and forth by waves, and blown here and there by every wind of teaching and by the cunning and craftiness of men in their deceitful scheming. Instead, speaking the truth in love, we will in all things grow up into him who is the Head, that is, Christ. From him the whole body, joined and held together by every supporting ligament, grows and builds itself up in love, as each part does its work. Ephesians 4:11-16*

Equip volunteers for their growth, don't produce copies of yourself. Equip them mentally, physically, socially, as well as spiritually. To do that, you must provide opportunities for their growth in all of these areas. If you do, you will see them grow into all that they can be for the Kingdom.

Each time you have a meeting take the first fifteen minutes to give them a tool for life or ministry. Invest in them constantly. Those times will pay off as your leaders grow up around you in every area of their lives.

Involve volunteers in bite-sized pieces of ministry and be there to bail them out, if necessary. Make sure that if they fail it isn't a fatal failure. If it is too big of a failure, you may never see them again. You have to learn how to facilitate their success until they can do it on their own. In addition, if you give it to someone to do, do not take it away unless they ask you to.

## Schedule Check-ups

Success doesn't mean perfection.   As your group of students and staff grows, you will need to keep your ears open to correction.  The larger something gets, the more issues there are that need to be addressed.  However, when correction comes, remember that it is seldom fun to receive.  However, if you learn to respond to it positively, you will walk farther down your path with less bumps and bruises.

Consistent daily devotions will allow the Holy Spirit to speak to you as needed.  He will point things out that others will never see.  Encourage Him to do that.  If you don't, He will do it anyway and He will recruit other staff as well.

Supervisory pastors have your work as a part of their job description.  Meet regularly with them and look at the future as well as the past.  What they have to say may not be easy to hear but if you have ears to hear, it will be a blessing and save you from future mistakes.

Parents will also give you input.  The only question is; will you solicit it or will they give it to you in the heat of frustration?  To avoid most of the potential heartache that can be generated here, seek their input.  Through anonymous surveys, parent meetings, and training times you can generate sufficient platforms for parents to input into your life.  Have these on a regular basis and don't just schedule them when there is a problem.  This will eliminate many of the unresolved problems that build over time.  When a problem does arrive, be proactive, not reactive.  Call parents first.  Don't wait.  Scripture calls us to deal with problems head-on once we have enough information to know how to respond properly.

*The first to present his case seems right, till another comes forward and questions him. Proverbs 18:17*

Review your goals and plans regularly. Have others look at your progress. Written goals are there to keep you on track. As you develop your plan, plan to work, and adjust the plan as necessary. Don't avoid the plan because you haven't achieved it but examine goals and yourself regularly. In one respect, you will be filling out a report card. Those are good if you can learn from them. Your openness to correction will determine the teachable level for everyone else.

Make sure that you develop the kind of relationship with your staff in which there is mutual accountability. Be ready and willing and open to the tough questions. Don't use the tough questions as a defense but as a measuring line by which each of us needs to measure ourselves.

Take time to schedule exposure to other ministries for you and your staff. Your version of youth ministry may be great, but it is not the only way. Learn from others since no one person has a corner on the market. Even if these people say the same things that you are saying, it is good for your staff to hear it. It is also good to be exposed to different approaches. That will give people options as things change and grow in your setting. What works today may not work tomorrow and everyone needs some options at those points. As you do that, make accountability relationships with other youth ministers.

In community settings, you should work as hard as possible at networking with the youth ministries that exist. Your capacity as a community group is great but your slice of the pie as a lone ranger is excessively small. Not only will you limit God's work with that kind of thinking you will also miss the watchful eyes of other youth ministers. Peers like that will see things that need to be changed long before anyone else will.

## Worker Maintenance

People are not machines and yet they need more maintenance than any machine. Remember their schedule as you involve them in the growing youth ministry. If you can help balance their lives in ministry, you will have long-term staff. If not, all the training in the world will only keep them a short time.

One of the ways you help volunteers the most is by your advance planning. The farther in advance you can schedule events, the easier it will be for them to properly schedule that into their world. Remember that they are volunteers. As a part of that advanced planning, make sure that you include times of rest and retreat with your staff. True relationships need unstructured time to go past a working relationship into one that is from the heart.

Appreciate volunteers whenever and however possible. Christmas, birthdays, anniversaries, and specially designed times are critical to the long-term success of your team. Notes, phone calls, e-mail, and public praise are all a part of developing a healthy team. Even though I can write this down in a paragraph, you will need to develop a comprehensive plan of how you can encourage the people that God has placed in your care.

## Remodels

Change is inevitable. As it happens, respond appropriately. When people have to move or quit for positive reasons such as a  call to ministry, marriage, or children, have a party. Rejoice in what has been done, who they are, and in the time you had together. Don't sweep things under the carpet and act as if it never happened.

When it is a painful parting, mourn. Eventually, someone will die or become physically unable to help. It happens. Mourn. Pray. Give the students a chance to work through it and give God a chance to do something about it. We don't have to live at the same pace that humanity does. Determine what is a realistic pace.

When sin is the reason that someone leaves, you have been given an incredible teachable moment. You must deal with it or it will deal with your group. Talk about principles and guidelines, not specific details. Learn to be proactive to the potential problems this may create. Be able to justify all your actions with Scripture and give enough attention to the problem so that it is genuinely dealt with. During all of this, don't lose focus on Jesus and His heart in the whole matter. Yes, keep going, but clean up the mess and let responsibility fall where it belongs.

Seasonal staff need explanation, especially if you have had some leaders leave for painful reasons. You need to help the students understand that seasonal staff will come back and that nothing bad has happened. Keep everyone informed and give them the opportunities to deal with the emotional aspects of a remodel.

 **Parents**

Every student who you minister to is cast in a mold that is created at home.  If the parents are moving forward in all that Father God has for them, then it will be much easier for their students to do the same.  If these parents aren't, then their students will have to learn from someone else, possibly you. (It's best if they can learn from home since they live there.)  You only get them on loan periodically.

Developing ties to the adults at home is a key to the fruit you will see in your work.  If things are reinforced at home that are experienced with you, rejoice!  If not, here are some things you can do to enlist the parents in the ministry opportunities their students will be offered.

To build a bridge of trust to them, you must do some concrete things.  Doing them will prove to the parent that they can trust you with the most important part of their lives-THEIR children.

Keep them WELL informed. You may have the best thing going, BUT if parents don't know about it, i.e. the cost, or the responsibility that goes with it, until the day before, you are dust. Informing parents means delivering a constant and consistent stream of accurate information well in advance so they can respond in a timely and appropriate manner.

Remember when it comes to finances you may have a number of students from one family. The number of students in the appropriate category multiplies the cost of an event for a family.

If people are not informed, it is always your fault. Find the ways that work in your world whether a web page, a computer generated announcement number, regular mailings, quarterly parent information nights, or all of the above. Whatever it takes, do it.

If parents are informed then, and only then, will their students have the greatest opportunity to participate. Once they are informed, then they need to trust you. That will take longer than the informational end of ministry, but giving them enough information will help you in *earning their trust*. God commissions parents as the primary influence in a young person's life, not you. Take the time to earn their trust.

Parenting is one of the toughest jobs on earth. Whenever possible, help them to be the best parents they can be. Offer parenting magazines, keep them informed of good books, DVD's, CD's, websites, or have periodic seminars on parenting issues, and return their phone calls.

You may not have the skills yourself, so look to those who do. Be realistic. If you are twenty-three your life experience probably won't offer them a lot. Bring someone in who can speak to the parents so that they will listen.

Sharing Christ with them will also be a very practical need. You will have students whose parents aren't Christians for a variety of reasons. They may be ignorant, hurt, Buddhists, or a local tavern owner. In all your dealings with them, give them as many chances as possible to hear the gospel and to see a credible ministry. If you can reach a parent, you will see a marked change in the struggles that your students will face.

You may also struggle with some parents who are church attendees but not disciples of Christ. When parents are not moving forward in what God has for them, God's call or a higher level of obedience, you will find that a challenging youth ministry can be threatening to them. Their goals for their students, and themselves, will not be in unison with yours, even though they may be influential people in the church. Their kids may see the hypocrisy and want out of the "church thing" all together.

Doing all the things that we have mentioned is needed to help these wayward people get back on track. You will also need to work closely with your Senior Pastor so that you can both work to reach these key people in youth ministry.

Parents are a vital part of youth ministry so develop your ministry to them as you develop ministry to their kids. It will pay dividends that generations to come will benefit from. Don't be afraid to see them as potential youth staff either. Their experience and passion for students, even if at first it is just their own, can help motivate them to be solid assets to the youth ministry. Often times at this time in their lives, assuming they are thirties to fifties, they have high levels of expertise in their areas of employment. Don't be afraid to utilize that or at least consult them when you are working in that area.

Until you are a parent of teenagers, do not imagine you know what it is like for them. Help them and invest in them at every opportunity. If you can help them to succeed, your job gets that much easier and more fruitful.

Here is some sample seminar ideas that fall into some parent interest categories.

- Anger and conflict in the home.
- Suicide
- Male/Female differences, i.e. *Men are from Mars and Women are from Venus* and their kids aren't sure where they come from, or *Men are Like Waffles and Women are Like Spaghetti*
- Planning for the college financial nightmare
- Discipline in the home
- Sharing your faith with your own teens; faith talk
- Relationships with teens in the good, bad and ugly times

A growing element in the parenting world is the home school home. These parents have decided for a variety of reasons that their role as parents includes being their students' educator. Because of that, their homes have different dynamics. Recognizing those dynamics will help you to work best with them. Because of their level of involvement with their students they need to be informed well in advance and with as much detail as possible. You will also find that they tend to have a better understanding of costs for events because they are already providing them for their students and you may have to justify things to them that other parents won't ask questions on. It may also come to the point where they question how much of the "world" you are exposing your students to with your methods.

For example, if you show a lot of current movie clips to make points or as illustrations you may hear from them. If you use secular music to make points or as illustrations it may be the same reaction. If you are just beginning to use these tools, send home a permission/information slip in a way that you know the parents will get it.

In both of these situations, you may find that other means can accomplish the same ends without endangering that part of the family of God. The message should never change but the methods can.

If you work with them, they can often become some key leaders because of their involvement levels. They aren't afraid of teenagers and often have skill levels that you can utilize in the ministry. Work with them so that you can have their support and potentially their expertise.

You will also find that home school students tend to have certain characteristics. First, they can be very outspoken. If they haven't ever been in the school system they don't tend to have their opinions crushed, so they still have some. Secondly, they will pick up the tendencies of their parents because they spend much of their time with them. This can be good, bad, or somewhere in-between based on the home life. They can also be easily bored since they move along at their own pace at home, not the pace of the slowest as happens in the public school setting. You may need to arrange a higher level of challenge earlier in a student's life if you have a sizeable representation from the home school world.

# What it all Looks Like

If you have gotten this far, here is what you are in process of creating in a youth ministry. Imagine a stadium with many entrances and exits. On the infield are the runners and coaches. In the stands are those who will probably be the next runners and coaches. Presently, for now, they are just watching.

The coaches have been training the runners, based on their past and present experiences as runners. Each crack of the gun sends off a new wave of runners. However, they aren't running in the stadium only. They only start and finish there.

After the start, their course leads them out in the highways and roads of the world around the stadium. While out there they invite people to the race and the stadium where the races all begin and end.

Coaches don't wait back in the stadium for them, they run with them. While they are out, they are inviting the strangers and coaching the newer runners. Some coaches run a lap through the stands of the stadium and invite the spectators to run with the team.

There is a gradual movement of people as new people come into the stadium to check it out. Some stay long enough to end up running. Others leave. Some of the runners don't come back as they go on to coach and run in other stadiums all over the world.

There are injuries to the runners. Some rehabilitate, others retire to the stands, others leave. Usually it was someone else in the race with them who caused the injury.

Every minute there's a new story starting and a new paragraph being added. You are a coach in the middle of it all. You are always looking for more coaches and recruits to run. In time, you may even expand your stadium or look at building a new one. Either way it just adds to your load of work. No matter how much time you have to give to this adventure called life, you run with your coach, Jesus.

Welcome to youth ministry.

# Training in the Classroom

"Talk is cheap." You and I have heard it said, and so have the students. In order for them to learn and experience the real race, you need to understand what it takes for them to "get it."

Jesus made sure that His disciples had made the transition from book learning to real life applications. His three plus years is similar in length to the time you have with a student during their high school years. Make the most of them. It will not just happen, you must plan to work! Get a plan, work the plan, and modify it for each group of students you work with.

| You remember | 10% | of what you read |
|---|---|---|
| You remember | 20% | of what you hear |
| You remember | 30% | of what you see |
| You remember | 50% | of what you see & hear |
| You remember | 70% | of what you say |
| You remember | 90% | of what you do |
| You remember | 100% | with the Holy Spirit |

Reading alone won't do it.  Listening alone won't do it. Watching alone won't do it.  No matter how you mix and match these methods you won't get above a fifty percent rate of retention.  So what do you do?  You do what Jesus did.  **GET PEOPLE INVOLVED.**

Jesus kept his disciples busy, learning by doing, so that when He was gone they could carry on with what He had started. This allowed them to retain it.  Consequently, we get to read about it in the Bible. Where our human efforts have limitations, the Holy Spirit makes up the difference.

*But the Counselor, the Holy Spirit, whom the Father will send in my name, will teach you all things and will remind you of everything I have said to you.  John 14:26*

You need to consider these learning realities in your efforts to impact the students in your care.  If you don't, you may wonder why they don't "get it."  You should in fact be repenting for the way you wasted their time. Your students should be able to say, "Did it, got it, do it."

In the Scriptures, we are told what to say. Our role is to learn how to say it in a way that students learn. This does not take away from our responsibility to pray for our students. But it does make it possible for them to understand the incredible book we call the Bible. Following are some creative ways for you to share God's word in such a way that they can't forget it.

*For I do not speak of my own accord, but the Father who send me commanded me what to say **and how to say it.** John 12:49 (emphasis mine)*

Take the time to learn how your students learn. Then your time won't be wasted as you do your part in helping them to be Christ's disciples.

As you use some of these creative teaching methods, you will realize that you need to start to "debrief" your students. Give them a chance to talk about what they have experienced and how it affects them. You can begin by asking them questions, and wait for answers, or if the group wants to participate you must give everyone a chance to share their observations in a small group setting immediately following the example.

After they have debriefed and it is obvious that they are getting the point you were working on, give them a chance to respond to it. What are their next courses of action? Truth without action isn't helpful to anyone. This becomes the "so what?" of teaching.

We have included five examples of creative teaching from our book, *Creating Controlled Chaos*, and how you could utilize them with your group.

**Event: The Nickel**
**Topic: Endurance**
**Scriptures:**
*"Because of the increase of wickedness, the love of most will grow cold, but he who stands firm to the end will be saved."* *Jesus in Matthew 24:12-13*

*"In fact, everyone who wants to live a godly life in Christ Jesus will be persecuted, while evil men and impostors will go from bad to worse, deceiving and being deceived. But as for you, continue in what you have learned and have become convinced of, because you know those from whom you have learned it, and how from infancy you have known the holy Scriptures, which are able to make you wise for salvation through faith in Christ Jesus."* *Paul in 2 Timothy 3:12-15*

**Supplies:** Enough nickels for everyone who may show up.

**Date Used/Group Involved:**
-
-
-

**Action:** As each person enters the room, give them a nickel. Don't give any explanation or information as to the purpose of the nickel. It isn't the main action for the gathering although it may have the highest impact. Continue on with your normal lesson.

• After about seven minutes inform everyone that if they want to keep the nickel they have to give you a quarter.

- After another seven minutes have those that still have the nickel stand up and have people laugh at them for about ten seconds.
- After another seven minutes inform everyone that if they want to keep the nickel they have to stand up and sing "Amazing Grace" at the top of their lungs for fifteen seconds (choose any worship song that the students may like).
- After another seven minutes inform everyone that if they want to keep the nickel they have to do ten push-ups.

When you are wrapping up your teaching or event then ask those who still have the nickel to stand up. Ask them what was going through their minds as they did what needed to be done to keep the nickel. Then share the scriptures with them.

**Application:** Serving Christ guarantees us some difficult times, just like keeping the nickel.

- How do we respond when (not if) it happens?
- Are we surprised by how we are treated or by what we go through?
- How can we look ahead and prepare ourselves for what we will face?
- What are the benefits that outweigh the hassles?
- Do we need to be forgiven for caving into the pressure?

**Student Notes**
Name & Contact Issue

- What are the settings that seem to produce the most pressure and how could they be turned around to become an opportunity for witnessing?

**Ministry Story:** Every night before we go to bed is like a dress rehearsal for our final sleep, death. One student went home after this exercise. He had given away his nickel as well as let sin seep into his life. He realized he wasn't ready to die or go to sleep that night. He couldn't sleep that night until he had gone to his parents in tears (a high school junior) and confessed his sin and recommitted his life to Christ.

**Event: No!**
**Topic: Hearing God's Voice Through Conviction**
**Scripture:**

*"But I tell you the truth: It is for your good that I am going away. Unless I go away, the Counselor will not come to you. When he comes, he will convict the world of guilt in regard to sin and righteousness and judgment"*
*Jesus in John 16:7-8*

**Supplies:** A blindfold large enough for anyone.

**Date Used/Group Involved:**

-

-

-

**Action:** Get a volunteer to come forward and then blindfold him. Begin to spin him in circles so he is not oriented to the room. Let everyone know that the volunteer "really has to go" to the restroom. It is really important that he make it there but the students can't touch him, they can only use one word to guide the volunteer to relief. The volunteer can't touch anyone or anything either.

See what word they think will work. Only key words work, "no" or "follow." You may let them even try to guide the volunteer with other words.

**Application:** Learning to hear the Father's voice is a growing need in every Christian's life, but it isn't as tough as most people think. The following questions will help people to see how they can trust that still small voice if they will learn to hear the first line of communication, "no."

- How many of us have ever felt guilty before? That's Father God saying "no."
- Do you think He says "no" in anger or in love? (love is right)
- Do most people love us enough to say "no" or do they just let us stumble along?
- What has happened when we have ignored that voice?
- Do you usually like the word "no?"
- Does your dislike for the word sometimes cause you to ignore or rebel against it?
- How can we learn to respond positively to the word "no" when He speaks it?
- Why do you think He uses the word "no?"
- Do you think the rest of the things He wants to communicate to us are dependent on us getting this right first? Probably!

| Student Notes |
| Name & Contact Issue |

**Ministry Story:** While on a mission trip in Australia we had the opportunity to do school assemblies. It was a rough part of New South Wales where the students aren't typically pro-Christian. This setting was very anti-Christian and our team was ultimately pelted with food, small stones, coins, plastic bottles, and incredible verbal abuse.

Wading into the opposition a discussion transpired between a group of male high school students and me. They were demanding to know why we were so stupid to believe in a God when there was none. As they ganged up on me in their verbal assaults, I let them know there was a God and that He spoke to them and that they heard Him. Again they hurled caustic remarks and closed in.

I repeated myself and asked them, "When was the last time you felt guilty?" It was suddenly quiet. Finally one young man broke the silence, "About two hours ago, mate!" That was God saying "no!" He would like to say a lot more but He has to start with something. Their silence let me know that they had heard and understood. From that point I proceeded to talk about what else He would like to say to us.

**Event: Hidden Treasure**
**Topic: Finding God in our World Reaching the**
           **Lost**
**Scriptures:**

*"For the Son of Man came to seek and to save what was lost."*
*Jesus in Luke 19:10*

*"And you, my son Solomon, acknowledge the God of your father,*
*and serve him with wholehearted devotion and with a willing*
*mind, for the Lord searches every heart and understands every*
*motive behind the thoughts. If you seek him, he will be found by*
*you; but if you forsake him, he will reject you forever."* *David in*
*1 Chronicles 28:9*

*"But seek first his kingdom and his righteousness, and all these*
*things will be given to you as well."* *Jesus in Matthew 6:33*

**Supplies:** A five dollar bill (or more if your crowd needs it to get
excited)

**Date Used/Group Involved:**

-

-

-

**Action:** Hide a five-dollar bill in the room and give the students
two minutes to find it. Most likely this will produce some quick
energy.

**Application:** From that participation level you can talk about
God's desire for the lost and/or our intensity to find God. Those

emotions can be built upon to produce a lesson that won't be forgotten.

- Ask the person who found the money what their process was that enabled them to find it.
- Ask them what process they think Jesus goes through as He seeks us.
- What process do we think we need to go through to reach those we know who don't know Jesus yet.
- Ask one of the people who didn't find it, but looked, what they think they did wrong.
- Ask them if they sometimes feel like they can't find Jesus and if so what might be missing in their search method.
- Ask someone who didn't look at all why they didn't even try.
- Why don't people pursue something even when it is possible to attain?
- What obstacles seem to get in the way of finding Jesus?

| **Student Notes** | |
|---|---|
| Name & Contact Issue | |

After this discussion and interaction you can do a teaching on how to have personal devotions or on how to share the Gospel with someone. It can be a springboard for either key topic.

**Ministry Story:** Brandon was on a mission trip with us in one of the poorer areas of Panama. We were working with the people who came to a medical clinic we sponsored. They often had to wait for a couple of hours for help so we ministered to them through drama, balloons, literature, and salvation bracelets. These bracelets have a five color story that is told by the beads they contain. I had shared Christ with dozens of people the day before with these bracelets and some had received Christ as a result.

That night, as we debriefed the team, Brandon announced that the next day he would try that same thing and asked for prayer. We prayed and the next day he approached the first person that came to us with a bracelet.

It was a young teenage boy. In halting Spanish Brandon asked if the young man had one, "No". Would he like one? "Yes." After he put it on he asked if he knew what the colors stood for. "No." Would he like to know? "Yes." Brandon told him, periodically referring back to a training booklet he had. At the end of his presentation he asked, do you understand? "Yes." Would you like to receive Christ? "Yes."

Brandon was shocked. He had never led anyone to Christ before. He looked back to his booklet and lead the young man in a prayer. Repeating Brandon's stumbling Spanish; the young man received Christ and was noticeably touched ... at least as much as Brandon.

**Event: Rubber Band**
**Topic: Fear/Satan**
**Scriptures:**
  *"Submit yourselves, then to God. Resist the devil and he will flee from you." James in James 4:7*

*"You, dear children, are from God and have overcome them, because the one who is in you is greater than the one who is in the world." John in 1 John 4:4*

**Supplies:** Using masking tape, or chalk, mark out a boxing ring size square in your meeting room. Have a variety of cutting tools (ax, machete, big knife, shovel, etc.) in one of the corners. Have a of couple rubber bands in your pocket out of sight, as well as a blindfold.

**Date Used/Group Involved:**
-
-
-

**Action**: As students come into the room they will see the setup and wonder. Once it is time to start, you can build the curiosity by announcing that someone is going to get the opportunity to fight you in the ring today.

    Once you get your volunteer, you need to increase the tension by blindfolding the student. To prepare for the point of this illustration you need to tell everyone that you have been practicing with the ax (or machete) and want to demonstrate your skill before the fight begins. Tell your blindfolded volunteer that you are going to shave a few hairs off their arm to show the group your skill level. Get a countdown going, and as you do, substitute your sharp weapon for a rubber band. At the final number, wet the end of the rubber band and have it hit the volunteer right where you were going to trim the hairs.

After the volunteer has reacted you now have a platform to show your students how Satan influences us with his most powerful, and frequently used weapon; fear. As you can tell, you don't want to let a weak hearted person volunteer. But you do need a genuine volunteer to have a realistic reaction. If for some reason they don't respond with fear you have a platform to ask them why. Their response will center on them knowing you and trusting you.

Fear also has an acronym that helps us to understand why we are subject to it sometimes.

**F**=Forgetting

**E**=Every

**A**=Available

**R**=Resource (His and ours)

**Application:** At this point you have an opportunity to share how knowing God's love will allow us to defeat the fear that Satan will use. Either way you have an illustration that won't be forgotten.

- How active of an imagination do they have when it comes to things that make them afraid? Things like noises at night, or a physical problem they might have. Get a few good stories from them.

- How often have their fears proven true? Get some good stories on what it actually was.
- How many have made some really poor choices because they were afraid?
- What were the impacts of those poor choices?
- Read the Scriptures.
- What could they have done instead?

**Student Notes**
Name & Contact Issue

**Ministry Story:** One of our students was very fearful of his senior year in high school. After all his Dad hadn't ever graduated and he feared he was just like him. Through encouragement he was able to finish high school, college, and enter into a life of ministry as a youth pastor. Fear could have kept him from the incredible life he now enjoys living. But with each step he took he realized that his fears were groundless as he realized who Father God is and the life He has for us to live.

*"For we are God's workmanship, created in Christ Jesus to do good works, which God prepared in advance for us to do." Paul in Ephesians 2:10*

**Event: The Race**
**Topic:  Conflict**
**Scripture:**
*"You were running a good race.  Who cut in on you and kept you from obeying the truth?   That kind of persuasion does not come from the one who calls you."* Paul in Galatians 5:7-8

**Supplies:**  Masking tape, enough for a race course with four lanes if possible.

**Date Used/Group Involved:**
-
-
-

**Action:**  Rooms, as we all know, are boring.  But many times they are all we have to work with.  Transform them.  Masking tape can create a cheap, temporary set for this lesson.  You are going to talk about "Running a Good Race," so put several lanes on the carpet with tape.  Then have students get in those lanes and have a race (younger group) or (older group) simulate one and see what some of the potential problems would be of a race on this track.

**Application:**  The problems we have in life aren't usually from people on the other side of the planet, it's from those closest to us; those who are running the race with us.  How well we do with them in areas of conflict will have a lot to do with our success in life.  You can use all of these examples as springboards to key issues that Christ taught about loving people.

- Who would be the people who are on your top five "hardest to get along with" list?
- Why are they so hard to get along with?
- What percentage is your responsibility and what percentage is theirs?
- What Biblical principles would apply to these people?
- Read the Scriptures.
- How easy is it to apply scripture in the middle of these situations?
- What area of your life do you think needs the most work right now?
- If you could pick the perfect kind of people to be on your track; what would they be like?
- How could you help them to become those people?

| Student Notes |
|---|
| Name & Contact Issue |

**Ministry Story:** Often those that are hardest for us to get along with become our allies if we learn how to respond to the sparks that seem to fly when we run on the track with them. We home-schooled our first two children, until they were ready for college. That meant they saw us 24/7. As our oldest daughter hit the junior high years she and mom started to have regular sessions of conflict that turned into arguments.

At this point you can't have two people any closer on the track. To work through the issues I (Dad) did the next whole year of schooling with our daughter so that she could learn some new habits in dealing with conflict. It worked. Having a year to learn new skills enabled the two to become very good friends as well as the mother/daughter combination. In fact, our daughter doesn't even remember the arguments and conflict. You may not have a year to work through things, but the reality is that you can get along with people if you work at it and do something to change things.

# Training through Preaching

Much of life is lived making choices from a menu. People look at their options and then decide. When you preach you limit the choices and end procrastination. When preaching is used, it should include the following.

- Truth and exposing error
- How do I apply the truth
- What must I do now to start the process
- A chance for God to verify His word individually with prayer

Jesus taught more than He preached. He taught when He was dealing with disciples and deciders, the hurt, the healing, and the healthy.

He preached when he was calling deciders to make a decision *(Come, follow me, and I will make you fishers of men. Mark 1:17)* or distracters were forcing Him to clarify truth *(You are in error because you do not know the Scriptures or the power of God. Matthew 22:29)*.

Whether you teach more or preach more will depend, to a degree, on your audience. Periodically you may need to preach for decisions, correction, or to call people to more than they have known before.

Periodically you may need to teach to give them enough information and understanding that they can make a good decision when you do preach.

When we minister in a Buddhist country, we cannot preach about Jesus until we have built a case in truth for His existence and our need for Him. Often you have to begin with a Creator God who created us for relationship with Him. Relationship was broken through sin and Jesus is Creator God's solution to that problem.

Students that attend your gatherings may know little more than the Buddhists that we minister to overseas. They may need a lot of information before they can make the choice to follow Jesus.

When Jesus preached and taught the Jews of His day, they were already well versed in the scriptures of the Old Testament. Yet with all that background, they still did not fully understand even after three years. Don't rush it with the students. I have heard it said that someone who accepts Christ after hearing the Gospel four to six times is ten times more likely to still be in church a year later than someone who hears it once, responds, and is then told they are ready for Heaven.

The style you choose for preaching will depend on you, your training, and your exposure to others who preach. No one style is the best. They are as many styles as there are preachers and as varied as the people who preach. I will include what I do here, just to expose you to another style. You can also contact us at www.finish-the-race.org and ask for an audio sermon.

I often start with a true story from my experience that will relate to the students and be a part of the message or get some information from the group that will do the same thing. For example,

- Luke 3:3-6 is a description of repentance. I tell a story about driving on the autobahn at one hundred and forty-five miles per hour. Students listen. The autobahn only works because *"every valley shall be filled in, every mountain and hill made low. The crooked roads shall become straight, the rough ways smooth."* Through the entire message, I can refer back to the autobahn story and then at the altar time, where God gets to verify the truth for the individual, I can call them to make their crooked roads straight.

- Luke 19:10 is a description of God initiating interaction with us. We are in turn called to initiate interaction with Him (Matthew 7:7-12 "Ask, Seek, and Knock") I tell a story about students on mission trips going through a buffet line in a foreign country. They have to initiate something or they starve to death. If they are too fussy or squeamish then they don't eat. It also tends to show up in their ministry capacity.

- 1 John 1:9 describes how we are cleansed when we confess our sin. I tell a story about a man whom I met after church. It was difficult to shake his hand because he only had one finger, his thumb, and portions of the other three fingers left. He told me he had come by a sliver and then decided to ignore it. Ultimately, he lost the fingers to save his hand. Sin left alone will not go away, it will only fester and get worse. It make Romans 6:23 very real too, as they see the death that the ignored sliver, sin, brings.

- James 1:2-5 describes the process of facing the tough things we must face in life. You can begin by trying to determine the King and Queen of procrastination in the group. They will have incredible stories of papers not done, school skipped, or duties undone. Once you have your royalty you can ask if that ever solves anything? Does the schoolwork go away? They may be ready to listen to a message that tells how to work through the trials if they face them. Finish the message with a chance for them to stand up and begin the process of facing their issues. Just by standing up, they will be taking the first step towards change and maturity. You could also have staff ready to meet with the students and help them through the process.

Students never forget the stories or the lessons learned from them. The Holy Spirit can minister to them when I preach as well as days afterwards.

A short sermon can become longer as you specify how the message applies to each of your nine targets. For example, in the area of sin you could address each target group this way.

*For the wages of sin is death, but the gift of God is eternal life in Christ Jesus our Lord. Romans 6:23*

- Gifted: Although they still have some things open to them they have probably closed some doors by past actions (sin=death to an opportunity).

- Disciples: Need to realize that God's mercy also takes place. Mercy means we don't get what we deserve when we deserve it. It doesn't mean there aren't consequences but it does mean the wages of sin come in the payment plan. They cannot confuse that for acceptance on God's part of the sin.

- Deciders: Will be able to see how their past is impacting their present. How the sin of others is not just limited to the guilty parties involved.

- Distracters: Will have part of their life explained, either their actions or others. It could well be that they forgive someone because of the realization that it will cost them more than the revenge they think they are enacting by their actions.

- Hurt: They can see that their issues aren't with Father God but with the impact of sin that others have committed.

- Healing: Can be shown how important it is to avoid future sin in their healing process.

- Healthy: Can be taught how to help others who seem to be struggling with sin. Principles they have learned from their own past victories and additional scripture (Galatians 6:1-5) will equip them to reach out to others.

- Adam: His typical sin issues can be addressed, lust, pride, fear, etc, and shown how to overcome them before there is too high of a price paid.

- Eve: Her typical sin issues can be addressed, jealousy, gossip, lust, fear, etc., and shown how to overcome them before there is too high of a price paid.

It is better to concentrate on one key point than to try to cover a lot of them. If students get the one key point then their opportunity for growth is greater. Imagine seeing students change fifty times in one year?

Again, sometimes we think there is a magical "Zap" service somewhere. With it, all the changes will take place instantaneously. Jesus never had one, why do you think you will.

Another tool that can help students is your ability to concentrate a teaching into a phrase, slogan, or acronym. For example, helping people to understand how to deal with fear we developed the following acronym.

F=Forgetting
E=Every
A=Available
R=Resource

As an underlying phrase to explain some of the key Christian life themes, we had this slogan.

No pain, no gain (Hebrews 12:4-13)
No guts, no glory (Joshua 1:9)
No sweat, no sweet (Luke 22:44)
No scars, no strength (2 Corinthians 1:3-4)
No prayer, no power (Acts 1:8)
No Jesus, no Life (John 15:1-17).

To help understand lust we used this easily remembered definition-too much, too soon, too fast, too often. When we were training leaders or others on relationships, we developed this one.

T=Time
R=Reliable
U=Understanding
S=Success
T=Tested

We have the most important information and opportunities in Father God's word. Let's learn how to effectively communicate it.

# 10 Training through Events

With a properly planned event, you can help students take some significant steps on the race marked out for them. Effective events will also become pet projects of volunteers when they realize that what they do with their limited amounts of time is significant.

If you target your disciples you could, in three or more hours, establish a key issue in their lives. For example, you want your students to grow in their ability in the area of personal evangelism. You can advertise this in advance and not worry about the other target groups coming since you have a specific target.

To maximize the time you will need to combine training and experience. Friday night you can give them the tools they will need for the next day. Then Saturday they get the chance to put what they have learned to practice.

Ideally, you can try out their new skills on people most likely to respond. You have a prepared a list of church visitors or those that have asked for a church visit or follow up. Once you have tested their skills then you need to take as much time as necessary to debrief the disciples on their experiences. In less than two days, they will have learned skills that can benefit them for the rest of their lives.

Your deciders and disciples (hurt to healthy) might benefit from an event where you go to a street mission and help feed the street people who enter. It doesn't take a spiritual person to feed someone. An experience like this, with a proper debrief, would help the Disciple grow and the Decider, decide.

In debriefing, you help someone process the events that they have been a part of. Often we associate debriefing with a tragedy. It's needed then but it can also be very helpful in the learning process. Students have 20/20 vision but not 20/20 understanding. You need to help them understand their experience in light of the scripture. If you will do that, they will have gained as much as possible from that experience.

For example, after you have worked at the mission, ask them to share with others what kind of interaction they may have had with the homeless. Some may have an incredible story to share from which others could learn. For some of the students they may find their life's work in your event. Others will realize that they can do more good than they realized. With the debriefing, everyone can learn from everyone's experience.

After a day of evangelism you will have any number of lessons that can be learned from the debriefing time.

- Did people experience rejection? Isaiah 53:1-3 and Luke 10:16

- Did people experience questions? Luke 8:26-35
- Did people see those they ministered to open to the spiritual issues? Luke 8:36-38
- What can be done differently?
- Does there need to be follow-up or training with individuals they ministered to? Matthew 17:14-21

For your Distracter arrange a fundraiser for a ski and snowboard day you are planning in December. During the fundraiser, you will work with them and get to interact at a completely new level.

Adams could benefit from a car repair day where they help fix up an old car orjust teach them how to do useful car skills. Your crowd might also be more interested in building a computer from spare parts for a local church or mission. The key is, it fits your student's needs and the learning characteristics they have.

Eves might enjoy a day of shopping at second hand stores or garage sales with the clothing going to local missions or a summer mission project overseas.

Hurt students needs to do something with good output but little risk. Have them put several thousand salvation bracelets together for evangelism or mission projects. Make sure they get to see pictures of where they go and the good they do once they get there. Use the time of work to discuss, talk, and build relationships and trust.

Healing might put the bracelets together as well but also get some training on how to use them and keep some for evangelism projects you help them plan for their school.

Healthy could work right alongside the others with the project while they also help teach the evangelism training and lead those that want to go out on an outreach.

Each of these events hits a specific target group and helps them take steps towards becoming as mature of a disciple as you can make in the time you have with them.

In the course of a year you should have specific events for each of your target groups. We all tend to gravitate towards certain groups based on our personal gifts and experiences. Looking at a yearly calendar will ensure that every student has a chance to grow.

This chapter is intentionally short as the following chapter on retreats is easily broken down into a multitude of individual events that are target specific.

 # Training through Retreats

In the course of a year, you can impact countless student's lives through retreats. Concentrated times with a specific kind of student and goal is the formula for major change. In a typical week you might see a student for five hours. With a typical weekend retreat you will have up to thirty hours and those thirty hours will be much more focused than the five in the normal week. You understand! You can do in three days what would take two or more months of the weekly routine.

Here are examples of what a retreat could look like for each target group. The goals and the method to achieve them are included in the plan. They are worth the work and all the extra effort that they require.

## Adam

Goal: Give them tools to deal with their issues and opportunities to be open and transparent

Friday:    Gather at church or Saturday if it is a three-day weekend and your Adams are active in sports

Cost includes five cans of food to feed the hungry

Travel to location and settle in. Location needs to be rustic if possible and not formal so that they can relax and do the type of activities that are planned.

Orientation:  Give them the rules and a fill out list that asks them to find people who will initial the box that applies to them (sample is in the appendix). Winner gets something that fits the Adams in your group. This will start the mixing process for your Adams. Make sure there are a few outrageous things on the list that only some of your leaders will be able to sign. Climbed Mt. Everest, etc...

**Event One:** Follow Me Exercise: For this to work you will need an athletic leader ready to run. Tell the group that they're going to play the game: follow me. You will point to the leader, if it isn't you, and say "*(name)* will be leading the event and here is how it is played". They say, "Follow Me!" and take off running. They will run a preset course but in four or five minutes end up back at the starting point.

As the students return, ask them, if they are ready this time. This time have two other staff ready to step in front of the students so the leader gets a bit of a head start. Have the leader run a similar course, but this time, make sure there are a few surprises out there.

Have other staff ready to lower a rope so the leader can climb a tree rapidly or swing across a stream, or other advantage. Have it available to the students as well, if, they ask for it.

After ten to fifteen minutes have the leader return. Call the Adams back and debrief. Ask them:

- What similarities were there between this event and the real act of following Jesus?
- Did the two who stepped in front of them hurt or detain them or just intimidate them?
- Are there any similarities between that and the devil?
- Is the devil more talk or action?
- Did some of the tasks seem impossible?
- How did you get the help when you needed it?
- If you didn't ask, did you get it?
- Now make it personal, how well do they feel like they do following Jesus?
- What are the challenges they seem to fail at most?
- What are some things they have learned so far in this adventure with Jesus?
- Have one of your leaders share some of their struggles early in their walk with Jesus and how they eventually won that battle.
- End with a time of prayer for each other.

Dinner: One of the Five Cans: After your Follow Me session, ask them if they are hungry. Their response will be yes, along with their question of what's for dinner and who's making it?

They will be making it and the "what" depended on "what" they brought in their five cans of food to feed the hungry. From my experience, food drives get the leftover and rejects of most homes. As they eat from this grocery store they will begin to get the message of this meal/event, "you reap what you sow".

For a variation, you can hide their cans somewhere and let them know that the group will be living off what they find in the woods. Their disbelief will be tempered once they begin finding cans, but then they will come to the new conclusion, what did we bring!

Do two or three meals from the canned food for the hungry grocery store. This dinner, breakfast, and lunch for the next day all take full advantage of the reinforcement factor that this learning experience will generate.

To make it work, have the first meal be things that can go into one pot. That may mean soups, chili, spaghetti, some vegetables, etc. Just use one can per person, with the idea that you want it to go together as much as possible.

Debrief:

- Ask them if they expected something like this?
- Are looking forward to breakfast tomorrow?
- Have someone look up Galatians 6:7 and read it aloud.
- Ask what percentage of their lives they think may be the result of how they treat others. The actual percentage is often much higher than what we realize.
- Ask for specific examples from the key areas of life
  - School
  - Home
  - Sports

- o Work
- o Church
- o Relationships

Have one of your staff share from their experience of learning this one, probably the hard way. End in a time of praying for each other.

**Event Two**: Spiritual Warfare: Make sure they are dressed in grubbies. Break them down into groups of five to seven with a staff member on each team. They will be outfitted with flag football flags and water balloons filled with latex paint, usually easy to get donated from peoples' garages.

The point of the challenge is to end up with as many flags as possible and as little paint on you and your team members as possible. It should be dark and some place where chaos won't be reported to the police or bother neighbors.

Once you have explained the rules and safety issues, give them fifteen minutes to disappear into the darkness and come up with a strategy and code words for their team. No hostilities take place until they hear the signal. After that, it is all out war for another forty-five minutes. When the signal is given again they come in to be judged.

Once the winning team is decided give them the necessary time to get clean and return for their debriefing.

- Give the winning team a food snack of some kind. That will be appreciated after the dinner experience.
- Ask for some experiences that can be shared. Make sure you get something from each group.
- Have people show their war wounds.

- Make the spiritual application to 1 Peter 5:8. The intensity of being hunted.
- Make the other application to James 4:7. We win if we play by the rules.

Now have another leader share about their struggles in the next level struggle as a Christian. The more open and transparent they can be the better. End with a time of prayer for each other.

Schedule some free time. This can allow for more interaction between students and staff, or be eliminated if you have gone overtime on your other activities.

Sleep

Saturday

Breakfast: One of the five cans. This time it may be impossible to mix everything together and still have it be edible. You may need a lot of bowls and spoons to serve up portions, much like a church potluck. In your debriefing of the event/meal you can ask what they would have done differently if they had realized they would be the hungry. It will reinforce their previous experience in the area of, "you reap what you sow".

When you start to debrief you may have even more input from your Adams. Some may be starting to get angry or feeling other emotions. Help them to work through that, make sure you eat what they eat too! Here are some questions that can help with the second session on you reap what you sow.

- Does it seem fair?

- Do you have to pay a price for other's actions?
- How can you deal with it knowing that others may mess it up anyway?
- Are you looking forward to lunch?
- What messages is your body telling you? Are they true? How long can you go without food and still be healthy?

**Event Three**: First Aid: Have someone, if no one in your staff is qualified, come in to do a two hour session on basic first aid. Make sure part of the training includes, "How to treat a basic cut and transport someone in from the woods." At the conclusion of the training break them into teams and have them practice the first aid techniques they have learned.

Lunch: Can number three: Again you will need a large number of bowls and spoons for the "church potluck." In your debriefing this time look at the aspect of breaking the cycle of sin.

- What does it take to break a sin cycle, repeated sin?
- Would they ever bring garbanzo beans to a retreat like this again?
- What are some painful lessons they have already learned?
- Are they looking forward to real food at dinner?

Assure them that they will eat a regular meal at dinnertime. Another leader shares on the topic of how they broke a sin cycle in their life. You can then open up for a time of prayer and response.

**Event Four**:   Use their new first aid training.   Have all the leaders of the previous practice first aid groups break a leg and require the team to find splint material and transport them a set distance to waiting help.  Encourage the broken legs to be painful and loud.  Let them know that everyone has to get all the injured to the designated location, which needs to be a challenge /struggle to do.

Debriefing them can cover a number of key topics (Galatians 6:2).  For this group let's assume they need to learn to work together and ask and receive help.

- How has someone helped you in the past in the medical realm?  You may have some incredible stories!
- How have you helped someone in any realm?
- What would life be like if no one ever helped anybody?
- How easy is it to ask for and receive help?

Have examples shared by another leader on these key questions. It becomes obvious that we need each other and that we need to be good at giving, receiving, and asking for help.

**Event Five**: Marshmallow Olympics: Now you will put them in a number of teams, 5-10 Adams per team, and prepare them for the Marshmallow Olympics.   Here are the events.   Each individual can compete in two individual and two team events. The winning team gets dinner, i.e. real food, first.

Here is a sample list of possible events.

Individual Events
- Shot Putt: See how far they can spit a whole marshmallow

- Target Shooting: See how many Lego men they can knock over
- Races with marshmallows balanced on their heads
- Big Mouth: See how many they can fit into their mouth without chewing them
- Push races: Have them push a marshmallow on the ground against someone from the other teams.
- Putt-Putt Golf with ... you guessed it ... marshmallow balls

Team Events
- Baseball with a ping pong paddle bat
- Wars
- Relays with marshmallows between toes
- Leaning Tower of Pisa: See how high you can stack twenty marshmallows
- Soccer

As this event unfolds, you will likely see unlikely heroes and unity or disunity. You have now created some "Adam" teachable moments.
As you debrief you can cover the following areas based on this event.

- Who were some of the most important people on your team?
- Does unity come easily or do you have to work at it?
- Why did the team who won, win?
- How easy is losing?

- Does any of this really matter?
- Why does it seem so important?
- How do we deal with winning?
- How do we deal with losing?

Another leader shares on the topic of competition, team work, and unity. Prizes are awarded and the winning team gets to eat first!

Free Time until Dinner

Dinner: Real feast: Make it as great as you can! Give them plenty of time and let them know that there is no hurry. To debrief from this you can share about Father God's mercy. After all, by all rights, they should still be eating two more meals from the cans of food they brought to "feed the hungry."

- What are some things they have "gotten away with" where there could have been some really serious consequences?
- Do they ever abuse the mercy that the Father has?
- Have they ever experienced something where the mercy had run out?
- How can being caught show Father God's mercy?

Another leader shares on the mercy of God in their life and their response to it.

**Event Six:** Grace isn't a girl's name. Pick two volunteers out of your group for the next illustration on grace. Make sure that one is small and the other is big and strong. After they are up front and volunteered, tell them that you have always enjoyed watching a good arm wrestling contest and that now seems to be a great time for one. Thank them for volunteering. People will automatically assume that the big person will win or there is a trick going on. It will be a trick but a very memorable lesson.

Build up the battle about to take place and go over all the rules of the match several times to make sure no one is uninformed. Ask the audience to vote on who they think might win. As the contest commences, don't let go, and the judge helps the smaller guy win as a real judge always holds the two hands together to make sure there is no early starting.

Thank the bigger guy for being a good sport and now share the grace lesson concept. Father God never lets go. If we will face our battles, then His grace, like the judge's hand, will be there for us to do what needs to be done. If we don't face them we will never know His grace and what we can be with it.

We are saved by grace and can do good works through it as well (Ephesians 2:8-10). That is why Peter's last written words to us were *"but grow in the grace and knowledge of our Lord Jesus Christ, to him be Glory both now and forever more."* *2 Peter 3:18*

Have a leader share how they have done more with God's grace than without and what life was like before God's grace. This will allow for interaction with the younger Adams.

- What are some battles they have run away from in the past?
- What are some battles they have won because of grace?
- What are some battles they could face again because of grace?
- How can they live life differently because of grace?

Break them into groups and have them pray for a specific battle that is ahead. Make sure you follow up on their battles so that they can learn to go forward in this area and not backwards.

Free Time

Sleep

Sunday

Breakfast:  Real food again. Clean up and prepare to leave

**Event Seven:**  Making a difference in the world. Put together a thousand salvation bracelets, or more depending on group size, to be used in a future mission trip or outreach effort. Explain the meaning well as you work on them and do some role-playing so that they can see how to use them to share the Gospel with their friends.

    **Black** stand for being lost in the darkness of life *(Luke 19:10 Jesus came to seek and to save that which was lost)* and what it is like to stumble through life not knowing where you are going. Get some examples from their lives and have the leaders share as well.

    **Red** signifies the blood that Christ shed on the cross so that we could be forgiven and leave the darkness behind. *(Revelation 1:5 and from Jesus Christ, who is the faithful witness, the firstborn from the dead, and the ruler of the kings of the earth. To him who loves us and has freed us from our sins by his blood,)*

    **White** signifies the light that we can live in and the purity of hearts that forgiveness brings. Father God's children have the privilege of living with His light and forgiveness. *(John 3:21 But* *whoever lives by the truth comes into the light, so that it may be seen plainly that what he has done has been done  through God.)*

**Green** reminds them of the growth that we can have in our lives through the grace that Father God gives us (2 Peter 3:18).  Then we will be like trees that bear fruit in time for those around us (John 15:1-8) and as evidence of our relationship with Father God.

In heaven the streets are paved with Gold (**Yellow**) and that is our final place and hope.  There He has prepared a mansion for us and things too good to describe.

Have another leader share his conversion experience and then see if there are any of your Adams that want to accept Christ now.

To culminate your Adam's weekend give them a token of their time together.  It can be a simple reminder or something elaborate but it needs to be something unique to them.

The Great Cloud of Witnesses (Hebrews 12:1-2) reminds them that this weekend will be a life-long part of the cloud that Father God will give them as a reminder of who He is and what He has done and does for us.

Serve Communion:  Pray: and leave.

**Retreat for Eve**

Goal: Give them the tools they need to succeed in their relationships, and be transparent with others. Have them bring all their unwanted clothing as a part of ministry to a clothing bank or homeless shelter. Emphasize that so that they bring them.

Friday: arrive as soon as possible after school.

Load up and head to the retreat site. Retreat site needs to be comfortable with good showers and sleeping facilities. Eves don't generally enjoy rustic. If it is too cramped, or simple, they can be distracted from the real issues of the retreat by conflict and discomfort.

Arrive and settle in.

**Event One**: Dealing with the failures of the past: Learn from the past but without being doomed to repeat it. Break them down into groups of four to seven. It will be a super woman contest where they have several impossible things to do. Make at least some of them things that they can't accomplish by themselves or in their little groups. Only if all of them work together can the task be done.

- Have them take turns pushing, pulling, etc. a vehicle a given distance, nothing that would endanger them, ie a hill.
- Pick up and move a log, large stone, or garbage can full of water.

- Throw a thousand pennies in the air and have them pick them all up in an insufficient amount of time.
- Hide a certain number of objects in tough areas and give them an insufficient amount of time to find them all.
- Hide the parts for a project that they must find and then assemble without instructions. They don't even know if they have all the parts or not.

As you can see, all of these are designed to frustrate people. If you have a number of groups in the four to seven size range, then you can have different events happening simultaneously. You don't want too much standing around, you need to keep everyone as involved as possible.

As you begin the debriefing process, the frustrations of this exercise will open hearts to some of the other frustrations life has thrown the Eves in your group.

- What emotions did you experience in each of these events? Write down the emotions revealed and save. This is great insight into your Eves.
- How did it feel when you began to realize that most of these activities were nearly or actually impossible?
- Whom did you find yourself getting angry towards?
- How much of life brings up these same kinds of feelings?
- What are some of the "no win" situations you have lived through in the past? Are you in any now?

Have one of your leaders share some of their past and how they got past the emotions of living through a "no win" situation.

Take some time to pray with the Eves and let them know that this weekend is a safe place to work through some things and get tools to deal with additional issues for themselves and friends.

Dinner: Healthy, it will help them to focus on who they really are and what can happen in their lives this weekend.

**Event Two**:  Have them put together a thousand salvation bracelets, or more if you have a big group. You want them to be able to work on them for at least an hour or more and let them talk freely. Go over the meaning of the bracelets and give them a chance to respond to the message.

*In the Adams retreat section  is a full explanation of the bracelet project*

Have one leader share how they came to the point of following Christ.

**Event Three**:  Make sure they have their grubbies on and have some Marshmallow Olympics. Keep them in their same teams of four to seven. Each person can do two individual events and two team events.

Here is a sample list of possible events.

Individual Events
- Shot Putt: See how far they can spit a whole marshmallow
- Target Shooting: See how many Lego men they can knock over
- Races with marshmallows balanced on their heads

- Big Mouth: See how many they can fit into their mouth without chewing them
- Push races: Have them push a marshmallow on the ground against someone from the other teams.
- Putt: Putt Golf with … you guessed it … marshmallow balls

Team Events
- Baseball with a ping pong paddle bat
- Wars
- Relays with marshmallows between toes
- Leaning Tower of Pisa, see how high you can stack twenty marshmallows
- Soccer

From this you will get some unlikely heroes. Have awards for the various events and lots of applause for the winners. Have a leader share about their success in relationships even though they aren't necessarily the social model of success in looks or accomplishment. Emphasize the area of controlling the mouth, gossip, speaking before listening, and loveless words.

Snack, eat marshmallow treats, what else?

Give them the sleep option or run a good wholesome movie with relationship keys in it that can be discussed afterwards.
Sleep … really! The more they get the better attitudes they will have.

Saturday  Let them sleep in and do a brunch at 10am

**Event Four**- Take them through first aid training, if you don't have the skills, bring someone in for a short one to two hour training. Then take them through the First Aid Kit materials in the beginning of this book. Make sure you leave time for prayer as some of their past wounds begin to come out.

**Event Five:** Take them through anger materials. Afterwards break them into their small groups again and discuss the anger issues that were brought up. Ask them what they think their next steps are towards dealing with any anger issues they or some of their friends might have. Anger materials written by the author are available from MST Ministries.

Snack: Good healthy food.

**Event Six:** Have them sort and repair the donation clothing they brought. You may need to teach some basic sewing skills for that. Pray over the clothes that whoever wears them next will come to know Christ and His life for them.

- Ask them how many memories came back to them as they were going through some of their clothes?
- Work through some of those with them.
- Ask how it feels to know that others less fortunate than them will be getting these?
- Work through the idea of helping others despite how you may personally feel.

Have a leader share how their involvement in ministry has strengthened them to deal with their own issues. (Hebrews 12:12-13).

From the clothes that are too worn or torn you can do the next event, bring some spares along, just in case for this event.

**Event Seven**:   In this fun event they utilize the old clothes. Break them down into their groups again.

- Give them two minutes to see how many pieces of clothing they can put on one person and have them walk. They actually have to be at least partially wearing them.
- Have them play Pictionary utilizing the clothing as the clues not drawings.
- Have them make a stretcher from the clothes and carry one of their members on a course.

As you debrief them you will be setting them up to move into the next event.

- Ask them how they think the clothes would feel if they had personalities?  Go from the new clothes on the rack to the ones you just destroyed.
- Do they ever feel like that?
- Read a short story of how they recycled clothing in World War Two.  Ask them if sometimes they would like to be recycled and start all over again?
- Get a list from them of the things that tend to overwhelm them and their friends.

Have a leader share how Father God has recycled them from their past to a bright future.

Free time if there is any.

Dinner

**Event Eight:**    Take them through suicide training materials. For the healthy student it is a tool to help friends, for the hurt and the healing it may well be for them.  Break into your groups and have them practice talking to each other as if they were suicidal. Suicide material by this author available.

Have a leader share from personal experience in this area.

Free time

Snack

Sleep

Sunday

Get up, clean up, and prepare to go.

10 am Brunch

**Event Nine:**   Happy Home:   Help them to integrate all that they have been exposed to this weekend concerning their relationships at home, school, church, work, and elsewhere.

- Failures of the past
- Salvation
- Unlikely heroes

- Movie topics
- First Aid kit
- Anger
- Clothing/suicide

Have several leaders share how they have worked out relationships in the key areas. Break them down into their groups to share, pray, and prepare for their return home.

Share communion

Leave with a snack for the trip home

## Disciples

Goal:  Equip them for personal evangelism and a big outreach you will be organizing later in the year.

Friday:  Leave A.S.A.P. after school.

Arrive and get settled in

**Event One**:  Have them make five thousand salvation bracelets and then go over their meaning.  Take enough time to ensure everyone is able to repeat the message and role-play with each other sharing that message with others.  Go ahead and give them a chance to respond to the message themselves.  Pray for any who need to recommit their lives to Christ or clean up their sin account.

_In the Adams retreat is a full explanation of the bracelet project._

Dinner

**Event Two**:  This is a teaching session where the realities of planting, watering, and harvest in evangelism are examined and then related to the lives of some of your leaders who share the sequences of planting, watering, and harvest that brought them to Christ.  If you have students that can do that too, then include some of them.

**Event Three**:  Have everyone there write a list of twenty lost people they know, non-Christians, that live in the area of your future outreach.  Once they have made that list, give them some general instruction on praying for lost people. Allow fifteen minutes to pray for those people.

**Event Four:**  Show a movie from a mission organization that depicts the impact of planting, watering, and harvest. *The Good Seed* by Wycliffe Bible Translators is a great example at about thirty minutes long. Debrief after the film on what it takes to do that much planting and watering before you see a harvest. Key in on the joy of obedience to God rather than the joy of success. Have a leader share an example of someone coming to Christ after a long time of planting and watering.

Sleep

Saturday:  Let them sleep in. They are often very tired after a solid week of school.

Brunch

**Event Five:**  Train them in the use of surveys. From this training, they will see how they can begin to interact with people and possibly get to share the gospel story they have on their bracelets. Have them role-play it several times and then head out and go to a place where people are and spend the rest of the day working in groups of three, one guy, two girls or two guys, one girl, seldom if ever three girls. You can also add some video surveys if you have the technology tools and people.

Midway through, have them get a snack and refreshments. Take a few minutes to debrief the group and share on the special things that have happened and then send them back out again. Regroup in time to get back for dinner.

Dinner

**Event Six:**    Organize the large group into smaller more manageable sized groups and have them debrief the afternoon's activity with a leader.    Have them share the things they learned and the things they wished they had known.    From these groups form a composite list of things to learn and things not to forget.

**Event Seven:**    Play a unity building game where they learn more about each other and learn to help each other.    Debrief afterwards and show how evangelism has many of the same elements of working together for someone's salvation.    One plants, one waters, and God uses another for harvest.

**Event Eight:**    Teach them the Five Key tools that all Christians already have when it comes to sharing Christ with others.    These five should help deal with a number of the things on their list that they wished they had known.    Find this list and teaching in the appendix.

**Sleep**

**Sunday**

**Breakfast**
Clean up and prepare for the next session

**Event Nine:**    Introduce the general strategy for the major outreach that is coming up, weeks or months later on the youth ministry calendar, for your disciples.    Describe the jobs that need to be filled to make it work.    See where people's interests lie and give them a chance to meet with a leader and discuss how they can be involved.

**Event Ten**: Have them pick three people that they will plant, water, and look for the harvest in during the next month. Have them pray for twenty people that will be targeted for the major outreach. Then commission them for the work that is before them. (Acts 13)

Eat Lunch and leave

## Retreat for the Decider

Goal: That they would see enough to decide to follow Jesus.

Method:  A lot of time to think, ask questions, and observe life and how it relates to a biblical worldview.

Friday:  Meet at the church and leave A.S.A.P., after school. Have them bring the funds needed as well as five cans of food to feed the hungry.

Arrive and get settled in.

**Event One:**   After they are settled, break them into teams of three or four.  Their job is to find materials for dinner.  Give them each a plastic knife and send them out into the woods, empty lot, etc. where you have hidden, while they were settling in, the food from their cans for the hungry.

You may have to encourage them to go past their disbelief and really look before the first can is found and then they begin to pursue dinner in earnest.  As the pot of food is cooking, have a leader do a quick debrief on finding things in God's word and how it can be done even if you don't think the answers might be there, just like dinner.

**Event Two:**   After dinner, have several Bible concordances, programs on computers, and study Bibles available, so they can research a topic from a suggested list of interest. Do surveys a couple of weeks before to find out what key Bible questions they have. Afterwards you can debrief on some of the Bible questions you have had answered as you searched through the scriptures.

Go ahead and compile a list of questions that the students want to get answered this weekend.


Free Time
End with a quick devotion and an opportunity for them to decide to follow Jesus.


Sleep


Saturday


**Breakfast:** Have them pick from the box of canned goods. After the meal have them debrief on the meal and what they would have done differently if they had known more. Bible truth is "you reap what you sow" and that partial information is dangerous. Have a leader share from their own experience of trying to live life from partial truths.

**Event Three:**  Break them into teams of four or more. Give them fifteen minutes to come up with five key internal team rules that will govern their behavior as they try to win the team competition before them. Give them the list of what they will be facing. Put the team events together so that they require unity, cooperation, and effort to accomplish them, for example everyone must complete it for the team to win.

- Carry a garbage can full of water through an obstacle course losing as little water as possible.
- Create an obstacle course that they have to navigate even though they are all holding onto the same hula hoop, or other object, that they can't let go of.

- Have them carry their smallest member over the same course.
- Have them carry their biggest member over the same course.

After it is all over and the awards are given look at the rules that the winning team had put together. Most likely, they can be traced back to a key biblical principle. Let them see and realize that biblical principles are keys to the proper functioning of any group, God's design for people, His creation, and works.

Have a leader share how they came to follow Christ and what Biblical truths were a part of that for them.

Lunch:    Have them pick from the box of canned goods. After the meal have them debrief on the meal and what they would have done differently if they had known more. Bible truth is "you reap what you sow" and that partial information is dangerous.

Have another leader share from their own experience of trying to live life from partial truths.

**Event Four**:    Do a major hide and seek game where some key leaders, ideally your former navy seals, are hidden and need to all be found by the teams formed the night before. The leaders stay hidden until a team has found all of them. Debrief them afterwards and ask what senses they used to find the leaders. Do a quick comparison to the senses God has given us to find Him.

- Sight: His creation
- Heart: His love
- Conscience: Guilt and His warnings
- Mind: Research into truth and it's impact

**Event Five**: Have a scavenger hunt with their established teams where they have to look for clues as well as for each item to find and the next location to look. Once they have completed the course, debrief them on what clues were easiest or hardest. Roll into a discussion on what clues are there in life for the existence of God, Satan, and a Biblical viewpoint to life.

Don't be in a hurry on this one. By this time, they may have some serious questions or want to make some serious decisions. Ideally, you can keep the groups together and have a leader that has been with them for a long time so they can work easier in their debriefing.

Free time if there is any

Dinner: Not from the canned food box.

**Event Six**: If they don't have Bibles make sure you have enough for everyone. Give them an hour or more where they can just hang out by themselves with God and His word and see what happens.

You should give them a couple of suggestions for potential reading, or how to pray, or where they might find answers to certain questions in the Bible. Give them a bottle of water or their favorite drink and pray for them while they are gone.

Debrief them in their smaller groups when they come back. There could be some amazing stories that come from that time.

**Event Seven**: Have a service with testimonies of what this weekend has taught them. Show them an inspirational movie, where the Christian life is clearly portrayed, *Chariots of Fire*, or one that hits your kinds of students.

**Event Eight**:    Free Time with organized games, board, video, etc. This can be some great interaction time.

Sleep

Breakfast

Prepare for departure

**Event Nine**:    Share a communion service with them. Let it be a learning experience, explain it a bit more fully than normal and give space for questions and answers and see how many want to take it. Pray for them as they get ready to head home and offer Christ to them again.

Head home. You will have planted, watered, and probably seen a harvest in some of your deciders.    Make sure you are ready to follow up on your new converts and their gold mine of friends, as discussed in chapter fifteen.

## Retreat for the Distracter

Goal:   To build relationships and help overcome some of the obstacles that these distracters may have towards the church and God.

Method:  Intense experiences

Friday:   Gather at the church A.S.A.P. after school and head to your retreat area.

Settle in and do your orientation.

Eat Dinner

**Event One**:   Get your group ready for your night vision ropes course adventure.  They will get their orientation and then head out on the rope course.  This will create a lot of stories and experiences that you can use to bring up the following issues as you debrief them afterwards.

- Trust the equipment
- Trust the trainers
- Trust the rope handlers
- Trusting God when others have already let you down who shouldn't have
- Fear of heights
- Fear of others letting us down
- Fear of what others would think of us

- Fear is **F**orgetting **E**very **A**vailable **R**esource from God to deal with the issues of life and what happens when we try to do it without Him

Have a leader share from personal experience of being hurt by others and how they recovered.

**Event Two**:  Have a major food feast with mingling games. It should be snack type foods that allow eating and mingling at the same time. Have them go around and find people who fit into a variety of categories that you have for them on a list.

- Someone who has slept in a car
- Someone who has been to another country
- Someone who has had an operation
- Someone who has a birth mark
- Someone who has a great-grandparent alive
- Someone who has been in a car wreck
- Someone who has a birthday in your month
- Someone who has the most brothers and sisters, including steps
- Someone who has the most pets
- Someone who doesn't have any pets
- Someone who has the littlest feet
- Someone who has the longest last name
- Someone who has the shortest last name
- Someone who has the most letters between all their legal names

This will allow you to get to know some of the students a little bit more while you feed them.

Run an inspiring movie such as *Remember the Titans, October Sky, The Rookie, Radio, Spiderman,* (know your students) etc.

Pray for them then send them to bed

Sleep

Breakfast

**Event Three**:   From the book of Titus give a short devotional on God's open enrollment policy. He accepts anyone and then will work hard on transforming them. In Titus, we read about the liars, gluttons, and evil brutes that go to that church. Let them see that the church will never be all it should be but that Jesus is always all He said He would be.

You can now debrief them with the following questions. Don't be defensive at this point, listen and write down what they say.

- What are some things about church that are hard to deal with?
- What are some things they have heard from others about their church experiences?
- If they could design a perfect church, what characteristics would it have?

**Event Four**:   Do a basic First Aid Class for them.   Bring someone in if you don't have the skills to do it.   You can now share how to use the First Aid Kit that we learned about in the beginning of the book. Show them how it will be helpful in the church as well as many other areas of life.

Have a leader share how they have dealt with wounds they have received in the past from a variety of situations.

Lunch

**Event Four**: Have all the equipment for a major paintball war. It can be mixed genders or separated into two groups based on gender or age. Once the rules and guidelines are established let the games begin.

Once it is done leave about half an hour to clean up and change before you debrief them on the following topics.

- Being hunted ... what was it like? Do they realize that they have an enemy who hunts them too (1 Peter 5:8)?
- Hunting requires all of the senses, which ones did they utilize for the game? What senses do they think they would need spiritually to be ready to live in a world where they are hunted?
- How did they accomplish some of the normal things of life like going to the bathroom under these conditions? Will understanding the spiritual battles that go on around them change the way they do the normal things of life?

Have a leader share a testimony of what it was like for them, when they were being hunted.

**Event Five:**   Do a scavenger hunt with clues. In their groups they will receive an envelope with the first clue. Don't give them all the same sequence of clues, ie.... send one group to clue number five, another to two, etc... That way they aren't following one another. Reward them as they come in by their place in the dinner line.

Debrief them by looking at some of the clues that Father God gives us, and others that are out there if we will look.

- Guilt: God saying "No"
- Able to hear other "Voices", ideas that don't come from us
- Creation

Have a leader share a testimony of their scavenger hunt with Father God.

Dinner

**Event Six:** Survival skills training. Bring someone in to teach basic survival skills for one to two hours for the area your retreat is in. When it is over give them a test for it; but don't tell them in advance, and see how well they do. If you are sleeping out that night, make sure the training includes building a shelter, making a bed, etc.

Now debrief along the lines of a life skills survival reality.

- What skills do they need to survive?
- Does the skill list change any if Father God is in the picture?
- What kind of damage can we receive if we don't have the skills?

Have a leader share from their experience of not just surviving but having an abundant life with Father God.

**Free Time:**   If you are going to sleep outdoors this night use this time as a part of the shelter building and preparation for the experience.

**Short Devotion:**   with an opportunity for ministry and prayer.

Snack

**Sleep:**   If you think your group is up to it, have them construct a shelter for each gender and spend the night out in the woods, etc. Let them utilize the new survival skills they have just learned.

Breakfast

Debrief the evening experience if you slept outdoors.

- What was it like being out of your comfort zone?
- Did you hear new noises that you hadn't heard before?
- How did the training you received help?
- What would it have been like without the training?
- How easy is it in life if you're not using God's instruction manual for survival?

Clean up and get ready to go

**Event Eight:**   Have your teams compete in an obstacle course. They must all finish together, still holding on to the hula hoop they are given. Debrief along these lines.

- Would the obstacle course have been easier alone? (Make sure it would have been IMPOSSIBLE alone)
- Who is on their team now helping them?
- Who could be on their team now helping them?
- What may need to change before they go home for things to work?

Give them a chance to deal with their issues, be prayed for and accept Christ. For those that did not, you will know them much better and have more wisdom to deal with their issues in the future.

Leave for home

## Retreat for the Hurt

Goal: The goal is to give them tools and an opportunity to deal with some of the issues of their past. This is based on a two night retreat but you could cut it to one to increase the chances that more people will come.

Friday:    Leave the church as soon as you can after school. While you are traveling, have an icebreaker game for each vehicle to help them open up and know those they are traveling with. You can use the same questions that are found in the distracters retreat under the mingling game.

Settle in with orientation and rules explained. Make sure they feel secure.

**Event One:**    Break them into teams of four to seven people. Have a riddle based scavenger hunt. Each clue will lead to another clue when the riddle is solved. Make sure they end up back at the lodging and that they can succeed, not mission impossible, remember your target.

Debrief and have a leader share how life had seemed like a riddle to them until they started to get good answers from people and from Father God. Give them the opportunity to respond to these questions, but don't force anything, again, remember your target.

- What is a question you have sought the answer to for a while? Be ready to get some heavy questions. You could also allow them to write questions down.

- Who have been some of the most helpful people in your life so far? How have they been helpful?
- Have you ever felt like Father God gave you answers or is He just a riddle to you?

**Event Two:**   Do the first aid training for them.  This can just be the teaching part of it or you can bring in someone to do the actual first aid teaching as well.

Have some prayer time with the students before you give them their free time.

Free Time:   with optional games for interaction.

Sleep

Saturday: Let them sleep in with brunch at 10am

**Event Three:**   Have a hide and seek tournament.  Set them out to hide and then keep track of when people are found and give them points for how long they hid before they were found.  At the end, give prizes for the total points.  If they stayed hidden this amount of time they get a prize, for example everyone from 0 to 5 minutes, 5-10, etc.  That way everyone gets something.

Debrief
Help them work through some of the emotions they may have had while playing the game.

- How much fear was there when you knew you were going to be found?

- What did it feel like if you were found first?
- What did if feel like to be found last?
- What did it feel like when you were a seeker? You can have a couple of students in each round help look.
- Do you ever have some of the same feelings in real life?

Have a leader share about their hide and seek experiences in life. How they used to hide but through Christ, they have learned to seek what their life is all about.

Snack

**Event Four:** Take them through anger training. Then give them a chance to identify where they are on the road to anger maturity and what they think they need to do next.

Have a leader share about their journey on this topic and how they are doing better now.

Take some time to pray for each person about their anger issues.

**Event Five:** Have an obstacle course set up that they can only work through with a team effort. Have them get into their teams again. Afterwards, have one of your leaders share their journey of learning to get help to make it through life.

Debrief

- What are some areas where you know you need to ask for help?

- Who are some of the people that have helped you the most in the past?
- What are some areas in life where you have to get help?
- What are some areas where you might be able to do it on your own?

Dinner

**Event Six:**   Movie Night:   Show some movies that are full of inspiration and truth.  Here are some examples/samples.

- *Remember the Titans*
- *The Rookie*
- *Cool Runnings*
- *October Sky*
- *Not Without My Children*
- *Radio*
- Etc.

Debrief that specific movie and the key elements of inspiration from it.

Pray for them and head to bed

Sleep

Breakfast

**Event Seven:** Proactive Suicide Training:   Take them through this material at a pace where they can interact and share.

Have a leader share one of their journeys through depression or one of a friend they have helped.

Debrief and pray with them.

- What stages have they lived in the most?
- What is toughest about recovering when you feel like you're not going to make it?
- What has helped you in the past make it this far?
- What have you learned that you can pass on to someone else?

Ask them about friends they might have that they could pray for.

Clean up and prepare to go home.

Lunch and head home

## Retreat for the Healing

Goal: To give them tools to deal with their past and give them some success in the ways of God. This can be based on a one night retreat to increase the chances that more people will come. If this is the case, then you would use a balance of active and more passive based learning opportunities that best fit your students.

Utilize the basic format as described for the hurt student but intensify and challenge them to a higher degree. The potential for failure can be more real here and it won't be as destructive as it would be for the hurt.

Following are some ways you could upgrade the hurt sessions for your healing students. This could make the events longer so you may need one less event. You need to decide what is most important for the students you will be working with.

This retreat follows the hurt retreat in format with some modifications to take into account the health factor that they have.

**Event One:**   Make your Riddle Based Scavenger Hunt a little harder than the one you used for the hurt Students.

**Event Two:**   After the first aid training have a mock disaster where the newly trained students have to save lives.

**Event Three:**   In the Hide and Seek tournament intensify the searchers. Raise their noise level or bring in outsiders that they won't know.

**Event Four:**   Add some role-playing scenarios so they can see how anger should or could be dealt with.

- Pick two as parents and have them confront their teenager, another volunteer, over poor grades. Show how it could go, a negative example, and how it should go, mature anger. Have the other students help them act it out each way.
- Have two Eves confront each other over a guy.
- Have two Adams confront each other over a car that was borrowed and misused.
- Have a student confront a teacher who is persecuting them for being Christian.

**Event Five:**   Make the obstacle course more difficult. Make it so that a wrong choice or lack of persistence could result in failure.

**Event Six:**   Only show one movie and have more interaction time after it. Add some more probing questions.

- Which character in the movie did you identify with the most and why?
- If you could describe your life with any movie what would it be? Tell us about it if we don't all know the plot.
- If you could be in any movie what would it be?

**Event Seven:**   Ask if they are aware of any suicidal students in their schools, neighborhoods, etc. Develop a plan to befriend and help them.

## Retreat for the Healthy

Goal: To give them tools to deal with their past and give them some success in the ways of God.

Utilize the basic format as described for the hurt/healing student but intensify and challenge them to an even higher degree. The potential for failure can be more real here and it won't be as destructive as it would have been for the hurt/healing.

Following are some ways you could upgrade the hurt/healing sessions for your healthy students. This could make the events longer so you may need fewer events. You need to decide what is most important for the students you will be working with.

**Event One:** As you make the Riddles tougher, also add the danger of changing the rules part way through the event. For example, if they start in teams at a certain point they may have to do the remainder alone.

**Event Two:** In your mock disaster include the fact that they have to transport all of the victims a certain distance to escape the coming floodwaters.

**Event Three:** Add another searching unit that destroys those they find, if the others don't find them first.

**Event Four:** Spend more time with each anger scenario and role-play it out in a variety of different settings.

- The family is poor, rich, alcoholic, step-parents, live-ins, etc.

- Reduce the amount of time they have to solve the problems.
- Add the police to the scenario.
- Help them see how they could be an outsider to one of these scenarios and help a friend work through one of them.

**Event Five:**   Make the obstacle course a little bit tougher.

**Event Six:**   Pick some contemporary movies that are a little bit more intense or that don't have a happy ending.

## Retreat Follow Up

When you have had a successful retreat, you need to plan for time to deal with the results of the event. If you don't plan time for follow up you will find that opportunities created by the event will be lost. For example;

- Your distracters or deciders accept Christ and need to get involved with some new believer's opportunities.
- Your disciples feel a new empowerment to do more for Him, so you need to have a plan in place for them to fulfill.
- Your hurt divulges all kinds of gory truth about their past that may need professional counseling. Have a network in place so you can direct students to people who can help, legal intervention, etc.
- Your healing tell you about someone at school who needs immediate attention.
- Your healthy want to use their new skills so you plan a new ministry opportunity to the homeless in your area.
- Gifted students reveal the pain of their past so you are ready to involve them in some recovery opportunities with counselors and a small group.
- Adams want to take some beginning ministry steps.
- Eves need to work out some past issues with family, friends, and the church.

These are predictable results when you know your targets and hit them. At this point, you need to have planned events and opportunities that will take this new dynamic in your group into account. Then you can continue to move them forward once the original event is over.

## Basic Retreat Planning

The success of your retreat will boil down to a few key planning elements.

- Plan it so it doesn't conflict with major school, community, church, or family events.
- Announce it as far as six months or more in advance, and make sure everyone knows about it because you told them so many times. Personally invite your target group and inform their parents.
- Budget as realistically as possible to increase your potential student involvement. You can seek food donations for the meals or "sell" investor shares to the people of the church.
- Make sure the praying "grandmas" have all the information they need to pray for your target group.
- Be flexible in your retreat schedule since it's almost impossible to plan the actual time frames involved for each event and the variable number of students who come.
- Don't rush through the event. Take full advantage of the teachable and ministry moments that arise.
- Get plenty of help. You need to make your load realistic and it gives students more people to connect with.
- The sooner you have it planned the better the chances of getting donations for the events.

# Training through Small Groups

Small groups will exist in your group. The only difference is whether they'll  be destructive cliques or constructively designed and managed small groups. If they are the latter they become a ribcage that protects the issues of the heart.

Cliques have been a feared part of youth ministry for years but they exist because people have the need for and the capacity for a limited number of secure relationships. If we don't provide healthy options they will exist in their cancerous form; cliques.

If we create and manage groups that have a limited number of secure relationships, we will have one of the keys to change in students' lives. The small groups can be formed around almost anything and in them discipleship can take place.

Discipleship can't take place in a big gathering of students and staff.

- Worship teams
- Gender specific retreats
- Grade levels
- Neighborhoods
- Short term mission trips
- Prison ministry teams
- Schools
- Events
- Bible study
- Football teams
- Baseball teams
- Basketball teams
- Greeters
- Follow up team
- Student councils
- Audio visual tech team
- Set up/tear down team
- Etc.  There are few limits here.

What makes small groups work are the principles that they live by.  The early church pioneered that for us.  If we make their principles ours, we can be part of small groups that change lives.

*They devoted themselves to the apostles' teaching and to the fellowship, to the breaking of bread and to prayer.  Everyone was filled with awe, and many wonders and miraculous signs were done by the apostles. All the believers were together and had everything in common. Selling their possessions and goods, they gave to anyone as he had need. Every day they continued to meet together in the temple courts. They broke bread in their homes and ate together with glad and sincere hearts, praising God and enjoying the favor of all people. And the Lord added to their number daily those who were being saved. Acts 2:42-47*

- *Apostles teaching*: Truth based
- *Fellowship*: Fellowship can be defined as two or more fellows rowing in the same direction. In other words, a shared experience
- *Breaking of Bread*: Eating
- *Prayer:* For themselves and others
- *Together*: Meet often enough to have significant meaning and priority in the people's lives
- *Everything in common*: There is no pecking order and no one is excluded for any reason.
- *Gave as anyone had need*: People learn to give out of their abundance
- *Every day they continued to meet*: Everyone knows what is going on and has total communication on all key issues.
- *Homes*: This is not an institutional or program realm. It must include the most intimate setting of our home.
- *Ate together*: Share quality time with each other.
- *Praised God*: Keep the focus of all that they do.
- *Numbers were added to them daily*: The natural byproduct of healthy small groups.

For a group to live this way it needs leaders who can lead them down that path. They need to have an understanding that this is the way it can be, if they lead it with Christ's principles.

Leaders will need to be trained and encouraged to work through the variety of issues that will arise as a group of students grow together. Denny Rydberg has a great book that outlines the key aspects of building community, *Building Community in Youth Groups* by Group Books. In it, he outlines the five key steps that a group must take as individuals before they are functioning in community.

They are:

1 Bond Building
2 Opening Up
3 Affirming
4 Stretching
5 Deeper Sharing and Goal Setting

In **Bond Building** you create a scenario where the students must work together or share a common experience. Once they have done a sufficient amount of this, they can move on to the second level, **Opening Up**.

Here they will a share part of who they really are. If they are **Affirmed** consistently as they begin to open up, they may feel secure enough to move on towards some **Stretching**. Here they are willing to go where they may have never been before.

As you work with students through stretching, everyone learns new things about each other. As long as affirming continues then they will be ready for **Deeper Sharing and Goal Setting**. At this point they are opening up completely to the group.

As you can imagine, this doesn't take place overnight. For students who have been hurt before it may take much longer. Either way, it is worth the wait, and needs to be managed in your small groups so that it takes place. It may not "just happen" otherwise.

Here is what it might look like in a baseball team small group format. Start the season with a "Spring Training Event" where you go over basics, play a long game (four hours, rain or shine), and finish with a meal (Bond Building).

Follow that with a chance after a couple of practices to go to the coach's house to snack and talk. There, everyone is given a chance to share his or her goals for the season. As those are affirmed and recorded you can help make a plan for each person that would accomplish that goal. It can be a baseball or personal goal.

Next use the context of baseball to stretch them towards their goals or insert some teaching time in the devotions that happen before each practice to stretch them in their personal lives.

As the season goes on, make sure you provide opportunities for deeper sharing and goal setting about baseball and life. It could be at a barbecue or during a baseball marathon you have to raise money for missions. In a baseball small group you could help your students grow in Christ in a way that changes their lives forever.

In the setting of a drama team, it might work this way. Have a training weekend to start the season. That would accomplish the bond building for all that attend. From that, you could sit down after a couple more practices and see if they have any goals for the season of drama either personally or dramatically.

As you affirm them in their goals, begin to plan ways for them to be stretched and reach their goals. It may happen during a ministry time, a road trip to train another youth group, or an overnighter at the coach's home where students get to the point where they are willing to go deeper, share, and set new goals that are more personal.

If the leadership understands how to facilitate this process your students will grow in their small groups. If not, then small groups will not be maximized and you will have lived through another missed opportunity.

You will also see that no group can or should last forever. Pick time frames that fit your local calendar and seasons. As groups are starting and stopping all the time; it allows opportunities for new students to get involved and for students who are involved in other activities at school, home, job, and family to still be involved with the youth ministry.

It is always better to celebrate what happened in a good season than it is to drag a group through a slow painful death that was inevitable anyway. It also means students can learn to finish something and look forward to another opportunity that they can now do because of the free time.

When you force students to quit, because the small group went on too long and they had to quit, you often alienate them with false guilt and self-inflicted condemnation. They are less likely to come back even though what you have to offer is exactly what they need.

Certain small groups will be open to everyone while others will be filled by selection. Other groups will be very specific in their nature, i.e. seniors only, sophomore girls, baseball, etc. Remember your targets as you create your groups and never stop training those who are leading these groups.

The easiest way for your small group leaders to "get it," is to model this kind of leadership through a small group where they are the participants. If these principles are established through their experience, they have a greater capacity to institute them in the small groups they, in turn, will lead.

#  Training through Ministry Teams

Student leadership learns best when they are part of a ministry team with a mature adult at the helm. We covered some of the potential options in our small group section but let's take a look at some of the keys to see students flourish in ministry teams.

The leader's role is to make sure that it works for the student. Students aren't supposed to be the platform for the leader, that means if it is a drama team, the coach isn't the star of every script. With that in mind, any ministry team needs to have the following components.

- Clearly defined commitment parameters, practices, locations, dress code, etc.
- Clearly defined ministry focus

- Beginning and ending commitment periods. Often a season of ministry is more realistic than a never-ending commitment requirement. It allows people to come in and out gracefully and new people to join an otherwise exclusive group. It also means you can have adult leadership that can only commit to a season.
- A meaningful ministry season planned for them. Details can be given to them and their parents for planning purposes.
- Training plus ministry opportunities
- Required reading or devotion expectations
- Be pro-active in your discipleship. For example, they will need to learn how to get along for this team to be effective. This can open the doors to equipping in areas of anger, conflict, spiritual gifts, and getting along. Don't wait until you have a problem to train people.
- A contract of expectations and requirements that both the student and their parent sign
- Opportunities to go through the five stages of building community in a youth group (for more detailed information see Denny Rydberg's *Building Community in Youth Groups* by Group Books)
- Planned time to discuss their devotions, lives, and then pray for each other in their personal progress with Christ
- Parent information meetings or newsletters.

Here is what a drama season might look like. Whenever you have a ministry team, you need to have a ministry plan that is on a calendar. That way people know:

- What they are signing up for
- How to order their personal lives, so that they can be a part of the team effort
- How it will impact parents and guardians as well

Therefore, your team leader needs to get some things on the calendar before a team forms and continue to work with a calendar once the team is formed. Here are some key things you need to take into account as you form your team's ministry calendar.

- Church Calendars will produce opportunities for your team and days you need to avoid. The ministry teams could help with a Vacation Bible School while you need to avoid an event on the annual business meeting.
- Community Calendars will also open opportunities for your team and you will find days you need to avoid. The ministry team could minister in the local celebration on the center stage and not try to do a fundraiser when the Kiwanis does their big fundraiser.
- Local school calendar, sports, days off, vacation days, fundraising opportunities, etc., may provide some opportunities but it will also show you the days that you will need to avoid in your planning. Usually you'll lose if you try to compete with the school. You are much better off to work in conjunction with it.
- Denominational calendars may provide you with opportunities as well as inform you of days to avoid in your planning. The mission trips, camps, and training they provide could be of great benefit to your ministry

teams providing them with opportunities that you cannot.

- Any other calendars you are aware of can provide opportunities and dates to avoid in your planning as well.

Once you have a basic calendar built for your ministry team then you can look at several other calendars that need to be constructed to take full advantage of the opportunity that this can be.

A **promotion calendar** can be developed so that you can reach your potential participation audience.

## Concept One

Promote and work out details-  June to August

Interested evening meeting - early August

Training seminar - 3rd weekend in September

Weekly meetings calendared

First ministry event - mid October

Thanksgiving ministry event - November

Mall outreach drama, children's  and/or youth event, New
    Years Eve -December

Month Off - January

Restart with Valentines Day Event - February

Outreach in other church - March

Easter event,  not large production - April

Mother's Day event, prison ministry opportunity, local parade -
    May

Graduation event, celebrate   accomplishments achieved during
    the year - June

## Concept Two

Promote and work out details -  March to May
Start -  June
Training seminar - 2nd weekend in June
Outreach in park - July 4th
Children's Vacation Bible School - July
Mexico outreach - August 15
See you at the pole rally, back to school rally - September
Halloween outreach with haunted house - October
Celebrate what you have done - November
Start up again in February with the idea of being together until
        June

## Concept Three

Promote for three months
Information Meeting
Start with training seminar
Six weeks of training then begin to do drama for Pastor's
        sermons
Every four weeks have another ministry outlet for the team:
        prison, mall, other church, etc.
Every three months have an improvement clinic
Every three weeks celebrate what God is doing

## Concept Four

You get the inspiration to have a drama team - February
You learn how to coach, research your calendars and ministry
        opportunities - March to May
You recruit and advertise the opportunity with your pre-planned

calendar - June and July
Informational meeting and sign-ups end - August
Training - September
Outreach on Halloween - October
Work in rest-homes/convalescent centers - November
Present a dinner theatre as a fundraiser or outreach,
    etc. - December
Celebrate what was done and the growth of the students and
    then begin to work towards next season - January

If your team is going to be a perpetual team then you need to start with the same kind of promotion calendar and time line but consider some additional aspects.

- You need to provide times for people to get in and out gracefully. Those times need to be a part of your planning calendar so you can secure people for a full term, until the next exit point, or encourage others to come in at the next entrance point.

- There needs to be scheduled celebration times.

- There needs to be scheduled training times. You will need to eventually provide several kinds of training, for the beginner and the more advanced people.

- Your ministry calendar should be ready as far in advance as possible. Giving people short notice for a ministry opportunity will create unnecessary stress as well as create conflicts that a well-planned calendar could help avoid. You will need to be planning for ministry opportunities that you are not even preparing for yet.

- You need to have evaluation times when people can express their ideas or concerns in regards to all aspects of the team. Are we doing too much? Do we have the proper time to prepare? Are our families suffering? Am I growing as a Christian or only as an actor or neither?

- Do you have the help to keep this kind of commitment and involvement going in a fruitful way?

Here is a partial list of some of the potential places where ministry opportunities may exist in your setting. Do your research about places for your team to minister.

1. Sunday school classes
2. Vacation Bible School
3. Children's church
4. Dinner theatre
5. Mission fundraiser—drama night
6. Youth group activities
7. Park outreach programs
8. Drama ministry tour—foreign or stateside
9. Drama ministry workshop
10 Float in a parade
11. After school care
12. Shopping malls during holidays, etc.
13. Children's ministry fundraiser
14. Youth revivals
15. Summer camps
16. Illustrate the pastor's sermon
17. Area wide youth rallies
18. Public schools
19. Advertisement for event
20. Worship starter
21. Street evangelism
22. Foreign field evangelism on a short term mission trip

23. Altar call
24. Begin a sermon
25. In a retirement home
26. Video to send to shut-ins
27. Prisons
28. Foreign speaking churches in your community
29. Fifth-quarter youth event
30. Church banquets
31. You and the Holy Spirit see what kind of a list you can write

# 14 The Gifts and Godliness

In the mix of all this are the variety of gifts that the church has been endowed with. There is no complete list in scripture but their variety (Romans 12 and 1 Corinthians 12) has both developed and destroyed the church at the same time.

Each gift has a mature and immature form. When the gift is immature, everyone pays a price. If the gift is mature then it is a blessing to all. The maturing happens with the discipling process that includes renewing the mind and comforting the heart.

*Do not conform any longer to the pattern of this world, but be transformed by the renewing of your mind. Then you will be able to test and approve what God's will is—his good, pleasing and perfect will. Romans 12:2*

*Praise be to the God and Father of our Lord Jesus Christ, the Father of compassion and the God of all comfort, who comforts us in all our troubles, so that we can comfort those in any trouble with the comfort we ourselves have received from God. 2 Corinthians 1:3-4*

Here are what some of the gifts can look like in both the mature and immature form. The mature forms are all characterized by a balanced life while the immature form usually is characterized by their lives being unbalanced. The list is intended to help you know where people are and where they can grow as they mature. It is not a complete list but I think you will get the picture from these descriptions.

## Serving

- Mature characteristics—Accomplish the goals of others selflessly, see needs and meet them, develop their own skills in new areas, as needed.
- Immature characteristics—Criticizes the goals of others, reacts to a lack of praise with bitterness and rebellion, will only work their way on anything.

## Teaching

- Mature characteristics—Clear in presentation, only shares pertinent information, uses correct vocabulary and understands the audience.
- Immature characteristics—Talks a lot without connecting information, shares all the background information that they researched to come to their conclusions, uses a vocabulary that impresses people but doesn't communicate to them.

## Encouraging

- Mature characteristics—Helps each person to take another step of obedience, positive and faith-filled in any setting, sees the purpose that every life has.
- Immature characteristics—They push people to the point of fatal failures and ungodly goals, negative and hopeless in any situation, see the faults in everyone and how that disqualifies the future.

## Contributing

- Mature characteristics—No one knows they are the financial backing, they work hard at developing their capacity to give, they give as the Lord directs not as their buttons are pushed.
- Immature characteristics—They have plaques everywhere and on everything they have given, they are lazy and enjoy the fruits of their gift more than they bless others, they give to their projects with strings attached.

## Leadership

- Mature characteristics—They see where a group needs to go and can plot a course to get there, takes full responsibility when things don't go as planned, can make mid-course corrections, takes the lives of others into account in the planning.
- Immature characteristics—They see what needs to be done and are afraid to act, they make excuses when things don't work, won't adjust to meet the changes that occur that affect a plan, expects others to mimic their unbalanced life.

## Showing Mercy

- Mature characteristics—Emotions trigger a God-oriented response, emotional conditions of others are readily understood, they have the capacity to communicate their sense of the feelings of others.

- Immature characteristics—Emotions determine their actions, other's emotions sway their emotions and actions, they isolate themselves because of their inability to share their emotional experiences with others.

## Healing

- Mature characteristics—Uses the gift at God's bidding and with His understanding, explains the ramification of a healing or lack thereof, can distinguish between the cause and symptoms of a disease.

- Immature characteristics—Tries to use the gift indiscriminately, doesn't understand or explain the ramifications of a healing or lack thereof, doesn't distinguish between symptoms and causes.

## Helping Others

- Mature characteristics—They see needs and are prepared to help fulfill those needs. It doesn't matter who needs help, they somehow are able to work with them and help them through their struggles. They are content with a job well done regardless of who notices or affirms them.

- Immature characteristics—They will see the needs but they may help just to get attention for themselves. If not thanked properly or frequently, they may become bitter and take their gift somewhere else.

## Administration

- Mature characteristics—Nobody knows you are running the task, event, or organization, they just know it's working well, they help other people organize their lives for success, chaos can become progress quickly.
- Immature characteristics—Everyone knows they're running the event, organization, and feel like pawns in it, they scorn others for their lack of organization, they bring order out of chaos at the cost of human emotions and futures.

## Evangelism

- Mature characteristics—They are as capable of sharing the gospel with anyone as they are equipping others to do what they can in the area of evangelism.
- Immature characteristics—They use their gifts for other means and belittle other's efforts who try to work in the area of evangelism.

## Pastor/Shepherd

- Mature characteristics—They are able to help people make sense of their lives and what they need to do next to grow.
- Immature characteristics—They are a control freaks in others lives.

Learning to live a balanced life is what allows the gift to mature. For example, if you are an administrator, you won't treat people as pawns on a chessboard if you are growing in your walk with the Heavenly Father. He won't allow you to continue down the wrong path if you are giving Him the time to correct you and guide you.

Bringing these differences out will allow each of your small groups and ministry teams to grow and work together with an appreciation that may not be there otherwise. You may also need to target specific events for the gift mix in your group.

If you have a lot of servers or helping gifts, you will need to plan more events where they can participate. If you have more leadership and pastor gifts then you need to create responsibility roles that they can fulfill at their stage of maturity.

As people develop you need to be careful not to pigeon-hole people into certain gifts that they may or not have. Every Christian will go through basic growth in each of the gifting areas. They need those opportunities to get the basics but not live their lives out in something that isn't their gift.

Environmental factors can also sway any kind of test results. When I take gifting tests, my activities at the time will influence the results. Normally my gifts test out as Evangelism and then Administration. However, if I have spent a few weeks in the office then it can test higher in Administration and then Evangelism.

Helping people find their gifts will be based on the opportunities they have exposure to. Give them those opportunities to find their God-given gifts and live them out for Him. There are websites with free gifting tests on them. Please see our website www.finish-the-race.org for a link.

# New Runners, Converts and Follow Up

Your healthy students will reach out to their friends. Those friends will come to your events and they will get involved. Many of them will begin to follow Jesus. At this point, you need to have a plan to take advantage of this gold mine of new contacts.

Most people have six to ten people they would call friends. They also have neighbors, relatives, and acquaintances that you now have a connection with. That connection comes through the new convert.

The new Christian in your group is very concerned about the spiritual life of their friends. You need to adopt their concern and help them to reach these people. If you do, you will find dozens of people that will come to Christ because of one who already has. If you don't take advantage of this short window of time, it usually disappears in less than a year and you will miss an untold number of new people that could be reached.

Your help will revolve around several strategies. First, equip your new convert with the basic skills to share their testimony, pray for their friends, and give them literature, DVD's, CD's, etc to give to their friends.

As long as they can plant seeds and water, you stand a good chance of seeing more converts fairly soon. As the new converts grow, help them to learn additional evangelistic skills. Help them find the answers to their friends' questions. Only about ten percent of all Christians have the gift of the evangelist. Take that into account as you train them.

Oranges never become apples, ever. Help them to find a strategy to reach their friends that isn't totally dependent on their gifts or success.

You can also put the people on additional prayer chains as well. Have the group and any other prayer groups you have in the church pray as well.

If it looks like their friends are hesitant about coming to the church setting then bring church to them. Have a gathering at the new convert's home where their friends will feel safe. Give a presentation of the gospel but when you use Bible references you need to do it by page number if you want people to follow along. Distribute Bibles, answer any questions people might have, and begin to build relationships with them.

You are now on the same page as the new convert and can work together as a team. If there seems to be an interest, schedule another time. It can be formal, like the previous one, or a game of basketball.

When a new convert chooses to be baptized, turn it into a big event. Print some significant invitations. Many people will come to an event like this especially if there is a reception afterward with food.

Finally design some specific events if your new convert comes from a background that is different from your normal student. For example, if you have a group full of athletes and the new convert is into computers you may need to broaden your base of events and activities in order to reach this new strata in the student population. This will also open doors for new leaders to help in a new area of ministry.

When you have your next new convert, don't forget to start all over again with them. If you track the connections that exist in churches today, you will find that most people, over 80%, came because of some kind of relationship with someone already in the church. In one local congregation where I served, we found that three new converts ultimately resulted in over one hundred new people in the church. One came from a large family, another had lived in the area their entire life, and the third was a recovering alcoholic who brought all their AA friends to church. In their cases, they did most of the follow up themselves. Imagine what could happen if all of your nuggets were followed up to the mother lode that each represents.

This kind of mining requires people, paper managing, and scheduling. Don't let that scare you. Having healthy students will be your best source of reaching other students. This will only facilitate that to a higher level. Each new convert is like a gold nugget. In Heaven, they rejoice over that one. You need to realize they're not alone and go looking for the mother lode. Mining it will allow you to reach people who would never have the opportunity otherwise to know Jesus as Savior and Lord.

Often they will be the fruit of a camp or retreat. Be ready with a plan to follow up on the new convert that is just as comprehensive as the one you developed for the event.

Have someone sit down with them as soon as possible and make a list of people they know: their family, relatives, those they work with, school friends, and neighbors. Work with them and develop a plan to reach this mountain of potential people who now know a new Christian. Pass those names on to your praying "grandmas".

Evan came to church because of a friend. When he became a Christian, his mountain started at home. He was the only believer and was mocked for his new faith. But with encouragement and help his whole family and a number of his friends came to Christ. It was a team effort that started from one brilliant nugget.

Don't just point them but prepare and encourage them. Be there for them when they hit the tough times. Have answers for them when it doesn't go the way they would like it to. If you do, you will find that one nugget can turn into a mineshaft that produces a steady stream of people coming into the Kingdom of God.

# 16 Calendar for a Successful Season

Things that impact students the most take time to plan. Therefore, you have to get good at working with a calendar. Jesus took advantage of the Jewish calendar in order to draw big crowds as well as be where the people were. You need to look at the church, school, community, and your denominational calendar in order to make the best use of the time available to you and the opportunities that already exist.

Working with the calendars in your world will allow you to be coordinated with them instead of fighting against them. This will increase your effectiveness as well as enable you to take advantage of some huge opportunities that already exist.

Number one, your church calendar probably has dates on it that you need to be aware of. For example, your church may have a children's outreach every year at a certain time. That can become one of your key ministry opportunities for the students in your ministry. It can only happen if you put it on your calendar and refrain from creating events that compete against it.

You may have a planning day on your church calendar for the upcoming year. If you aren't ready with your plans by that date you may not have anything to do in the future year. Be very aware of that and be prepared, having taken into account all the other calendar dates.

Second, your local school may be the most influential calendar in the community. Find out when the vacations, key-sporting events, parent nights, etc., are happening. Working with these dates will enable you to see your students more often at your events. Some school events can also double as one of your events. Make a certain football game an outreach event where you and your students distribute tracts, with a football player's testimony on them, or do an after-game event and pass out invitations at the game.

If your students are involved in school activities, go and see them in their normal environment. Players, cheerleaders, band members, and photographers may all attend your church. Being there for an event may allow you to see them and meet many of their friends. Don't fight the school calendar, but if a school event isn't appropriate, then you could schedule an alternative event.

You can also take full advantage of the vacations that each school system has. Normally there is summer break, spring and winter breaks, three-day weekends, mid-winter break, and teacher training days, etc. By planning something you help parents who may not have those days off (student babysitting), as well as maximize that time for them and the Kingdom of God.

Next, your community has a calendar too. There are certain days when they have parades, community festivals, or some kind of fundraising focus. Find out how you can be a ministering force or a fundraising magnet during those times. Planning will allow you to maximize these opportunities.

Fourth, each denomination has planned events for the students in their denomination. Find out the what, when, where, why, how much, and registration information for these events. Then you can work with those dates as well. What you don't know can hurt you when it comes to planning and taking advantage of what is already out there.

Finally, don't forget your personal calendar. You need to make sure your family is even more nourished than your ministry people. That won't happen if you don't plan those special anniversaries and vacations into the calendar. Also, if you aren't married yet, avoid key youth ministry times when you do get married so you can keep that day special for the lifetime of anniversaries you should plan on having.

Once you have your possible menu you need to start planning with certain factors in mind. You have a variety of students you are ministering to. You need to take these factors into account as you plan.

First, you, hopefully, have students that want to be there, disciples. They are honestly trying to follow Jesus. In the course of a year, they need events that will encourage them, train them, and challenge them in the ways of Christ.

Second, you have other students that have to be there, distracters. Someone else has made the decision for them. They need events that give them an opportunity to receive Christ as well as events they want to come to because they're awesome events. You can give them a chance to respond to the Gospel at an awesome event and take care of the two needs together. Your students that want to be there will probably enjoy these as well and they'll know that they can bring their lost friends to these events.

244     Finish the Race – Know the Course

Third, you will have some students who come and you don't know why they come, deciders. Somehow they just show up very regularly. They need to have a calendar in front of them so that they can come and find Christ and grow. As you plan you need to balance your calendar so that all the students get enough opportunities to grow in Christ or come to Him.

Fourth, you have Adams, guys who need some specific opportunities to grow in their common areas of struggle. They need to be separated from the ladies to open up and grow.

Fifth, you have Eves, ladies, who also need specific opportunities to grow in their common areas of struggle. They need to be separate from the guys to open up and grow. Understanding the health of your group, hurt, healing, and healthy, also needs to be taken into account as you plan your calendars.

Keep your calendars on file, so that you can see what you have done and build off each success. Certain students will love certain events. Spread their use around to avoid over-use.

If an event fails, find out why. Did you compete with another event and lose? Maybe you didn't advertise well enough?

For students to come you need to tell them six times at least three different ways well in advance. Use whatever means are available to get students and their parents informed and a part of the event. You need a promotion calendar that you work from as well as an event calendar that you distribute.

Once you have your planning calendar done then you can move on to your promotion calendar. It may look something like this.

## Sample Promotion Calendar Sequences

You've picked **July 7-11** for your summer camp. Promotion dates begin in December. Regular mailings and announcements begin then. Be creative in your use of your six times done at least three different ways. Don't forget the parents who will need to plan vacation and finances for your camp. Registration deadline is June 5 so announce it as June 1 to make sure you have all the paper work in order before it has to be postmarked.

Each significant event will need work like this. Therefore, you will have to decide which events are significant for the students and work the promotion angle well. Keeping them informed will minimize your frustration of having an ill-attended awesome event.

As I travel and minister I have encountered numerous situations where a great event was planned but the participation was poor because no one took the time to promote it properly.

A sample yearly calendar might look like this:

**January**- Winter camp-Focus of evangelism with options for the discipleship students too.
**February**- Alternative Valentine's celebration-Focus of discipleship for students trying to follow Jesus.
**March**- Fun events with focus on evangelism, the students in any of your categories would come.
**April**- An evangelism outreach over the public school holiday. Take new converts and discipleship students on a four day outreach in the local area. This is a good discipleship time and training for summer mission trips.

**May-** Spring sports start up. Focus on reaching the deciders and distracters as well as their friends.

**June-** School graduations and alternative parties. Last chance to reach your students who haven't come to Christ and celebrate with those who are moving on towards their post high school careers.

**July-** Camp month-Get all your students to camp, some for salvation, others for growth, and others for fellowship.

**August-** Mission month-Get as many students to go as possible (disciples).

**September-** Get them ready for school. Have training for Christians to minister on campus as well as preparing them for the pressures they haven't had all summer.

**October-** Fun alternatives to Halloween that can also be outreach oriented.

**November-** Thanksgiving feed the hungry projects, geared towards growing your disciples.

**December-** Outreach at Christmas break for your disciples as well as some fun events to maintain contacts with the deciders and distracters.

On a weekly basis, you might structure one of your meetings towards discipleship and another towards outreach and the lost. We ended up having mostly disciples on our mid-week service and many deciders and distracters on Sunday morning. These two weekly events were very different but hit their specific targets.

This is a sample of how you can minister to the variety of students that you will have if you plan. It will allow you to see them all grow and bring their friends along. Most numerical growth comes through reaching someone who has friends who don't go to church, yet. Proper planning will allow you to maximize that.

Following is an example if you are in a small youth group setting and you don't have much time or resources, yet you have a few of each of these kinds of students in your group.

**January-** Go on a winter camp with another group. Find out their focus and make that yours too.

**February-** Have a meal at your house around Valentine's Day and talk about how you and your wife get along and why your marriage works. Many students are in desperate need of seeing that marriages can work and are worth striving for. If you are single, find a solid couple in the church who would do the honors.

**March-** Take the students camping in the church. It can be very low budget and get donations from the people of the church for food. Make it a combination of fun and outreach for the lost students who come.

**April-** During a school holiday have a day where they do spring cleaning in homes and yards of the elderly in the church. Take some time afterwards to see what other projects they think they could do for God in the future. Write them down and when possible include them in future plans.

**May-** Make May a month where you bring someone in to do training with your students for a summer mission trip. Plan it with someone else who is already going. Many youth groups do a summer outreach and many denominations provide programs for this kind of situation. Get to know some of the leadership so you can send your students with confidence.

**June-** Celebrate graduates and have a moving forward event where you focus on how students can make good decisions for their future.

**July-** Send as many students to camp as you can.

**August-** Send as many students as you can on the mission trip you selected. While they are gone on the mission trip, have a fun day for the others who didn't go.

**September-** Have a back to school retreat at your house and get them ready for school to minister or just face the trouble that will be there to face them.

**October-** Have an outreach based on the spiritual realities of Halloween and what it has become. Make it an outreach night and alternative to the normal chaos.

**November-** Have a planned famine time where you adopt an orphan somewhere in the world based on your thankfulness for having so much here in your country.

**December-** Do a Christmas musical that you can do in the church, rest homes, local jails and anywhere else you have opportunities.

## Winter Camp Planning Timetables

With these in mind, let's work through some realistic timetables for three typical events in youth ministry. First, let's go to Winter Camp on January 22-24 and it costs $89.00. You need to let people know about the dates as soon as they are confirmed. Place a short note in the next newsletter. A year in advance isn't too far in advance.

Remember, if a family has three kids in the youth group that is almost $300.00 for them. Keep it on every newsletter you have until the event arrives. Put it on your web site and update it as you get details.

Have a registration and permission form ready as soon as you make the dates known. It doesn't have to have everything on it, but it is a way for students to start to pay for it in advance.

Have a bookkeeping system that allows people to pay for their events in advance.

Once a month have a student share a quick testimony of what camp was like last year. Get the pictures and video footage out every other month and remind them of what God can do at a time like this.

Start pushing for registrations in September, even if it competes with other events. You don't want to let this one be missed by your students. In September start a parent sign up for a prayer chain that will pray while you are at camp. Solicit scholarship funds from the church body and make them available as needed. If possible, have your camp speaker minister to your students in a mid-week service a couple of months before camp. This helps the camp to start at a better pace and is great advertising.

Continue to collect money and have the detail of the camp activities ready to hand out as needed. Make calls to anyone who isn't moving in the camp direction and see if there is a problem that exists and can be worked out. It may be money, it may be a parent issue, or it may be a school conflict. Find out why students aren't going and make any adjustments that you can for this year. Use this information to make any changes for next year.

Go to winter camp and plan to have at least 80% of your students there. That will change your youth group. Events like this have a capacity to advance what God is doing in individual lives and in the youth group much faster than any sermon, so invest the time it takes to do a "no regrets" job.

## Mexico Mission Trip

Now let's go to Mexico in August. This will require even more advance planning. You need to have the dates and costs nailed down before November of the preceding year (budget sheet sample is in the Appendix). With the advance notice, your youth staff can get the days off from work to go with you and parents won't schedule family vacations on the same dates.

Communicate a large trip like this to the whole church on a regular basis. As you communicate, don't say anything that might change. Every flyer you produce needs to agree on dates, prices, and requirements. Have several people proofread things so you don't destroy your budget process with bad information.

Plan it so there are no large conflicts with other ministries in the church. If your dates conflict with too many groups you lose some of the support you could have had from the church. This also allows people to participate financially and in prayer.

Have informational meetings for your parents and students long before you have financial deadlines. You should be able to answer most of the questions because you have already been there on a set up trip, (sample setup trip information list is in the Appendix). Parents won't send their students or support you if there is an unnecessary element of risk or uncertainty.

Start the money collection process as soon as you announce the trip. Give the students a chance to give you money every time you meet. Don't rely on a single strategy to see the finances come in. First, encourage the students to sacrifice. A lot of money passes through their hands. Make sure it goes where it belongs. Second, encourage them to work in any setting that doesn't compromise their walk with Jesus.

Third, make sure they work in any fundraising opportunities that are planned. Don't rely on fundraisers but don't neglect them either. Group garage sales, candy bars, calendars, etc, and personal sales can generate substantial amounts of funds. David picked up five stones when he attacked Goliath. He only needed one; you may need all five.

Fourth, develop an asking strategy. Letters to family members, local businesses, church friends, and relatives can help expand those who participate. Some students may fund their entire trip this way while others will not receive much at all.

Fifth, sell something they own. They may have a small fortune invested in something(s) that they can sell. I've seen more than one student finance a trip this way.

Use this focus as a way to raise the discipleship standard in your group. When they go, they will be changed. Start the change process before they leave all the natural ministry connections that exist in your area of ministry.

Public school campus clubs should be strengthened as your future missionaries minister in their local setting before they leave their backyard and minister.

As you pour all this energy and planning into the Mexico mission trip, remember that not everyone will go. Have a good plan for those that don't go while you are gone and don't forget those that aren't going as you prepare with those who are.

If those who stay behind have a bad experience while you are having a good one, they won't consider going next year. They may not even stick around long enough to go in the future.

When you return, have a plan to utilize all the students who will be excited and ready to continue to be involved in ministry opportunities. Don't get them all excited and then leave them stranded. Equip them for a local Vacation Bible School or ministry for the next school year. Even though it is a big event, it is only one event and it will only be available to some of your students.

Do a large presentation for the congregation and send reports and pictures to anyone who helped support the team or its members. You can build your support base for years to come if you let those who help the first time know how much they are appreciated.

## Simple Skate Night

All the details need to be out at least a month in advance. If they aren't, you will miss out on an incredible opportunity to reach new students and build the youth group into a solid growing community. Advertise it regularly and don't stop until the event arrives.

Even though you can announce an event like this only a month in advance it needs to be on your yearly planning calendar a year in advance. Each event you schedule needs to fit into a plan that is producing disciples and giving them a chance to be involved in ministry opportunities. Get good at yearly planning, two-year plans, and advance planning that scares you.

Have a way to track your students that come as well as the visitors. If they come and have a positive experience, it will be easier to invite them to something else. If you don't have an address or phone number you will miss what could happen from a simple event. Every student knows another student and you can reach the entire world from one person (assuming you had enough time). Your permission slips should provide you with that (see Appendix) and you need to have a system established to add these new people to your mailing lists.

Like any event, you get out of it what you put into it. Therefore, prayer and fasting can be just as appropriate for this event as it is for the Winter Camp. Have some time after the event so you can follow through on your new contacts.

## In Summary

After all the planning that we just talked about, be flexible enough to take advantage of things that happen that can't be predicted. Local flooding, a fire in an apartment complex, power outages, or a lost child can all be opportunities to mobilize the army of God that you are developing for ministry opportunities. This requires that you keep abreast of the local news and stay tuned to your community's heartbeat.

Jesus had a plan and followed it until His death. He also had enough time to minister despite the interruptions that came up as people all around Him found themselves in need. From the woman who touched His garment to the man who came because of his dying daughter, Jesus made the time for them. If you have developed a strong communication system, then you can take advantage of the unplanned opportunities. If you haven't, you can't.

As you can see, the calendar should be your best friend at this point. Don't compete for the loyalties of your students or their families until you are big enough and established enough to win. Forcing students to choose too early in their discipleship period just because you didn't look at a calendar soon enough is not wise. In time, you may have enough influence to have the schools calling you. Until then, call them and get their dates.

Advance planning will also allow people to be involved in advanced financing. Paul would tell the people in advance of a visit that he was going to take an offering when he arrived.

*And here is my advice about what is best for you in this matter: Last year you were the first not only to give but also to have the desire to do so. Now finish the work, so that your eager willingness to do it may be matched by your completion of it, according to your means. For if the willingness is there, the gift is acceptable according to what one has, not according to what he does not have. Our desire is not that others might be relieved while you are hard pressed, but that there might be equality. At the present time your plenty will supply what they need, so that in turn their plenty will supply what you need. Then there will be equality, as it is written: He who gathered much did not have too much, and he who gathered little did not have too little.   2 Corinthians 8:10-15*

This allowed them to set aside money so that when he came they could participate in the giving--joyfully.

If you surprise people with costly events they may still give, but it won't be joyfully. In time, you will wear out your welcome in the area of costly events. Instead, if you plan well and notify everyone in advance, then you will see people planning to participate and setting aside the finances that are needed for your event.

Advance planning will also make it possible for your volunteers to be a key part of the ministry. You can use an army of two to five hour a week people if you give them enough advance notice of their opportunities. Without that, you may find yourself working alone.

 # Communication is Coordination

We (the church) have the best thing going, but too often, nobody knows about it. Don't let all your prayers, planning, and time be wasted because you didn't get the word out soon enough. This is so important that you are better off doing less and having it well attended than doing more and wondering where everyone was.

There is a basic rule to remember when you really want people to be a part of your activity. Tell them six different times at least three different ways with an appropriate amount of advance warning. The more money or time involved the more advance communication needed.

There are more ways to communicate now than there ever have been before. Make sure you learn to utilize them so that those who need to hear will have the opportunity. Then establish realistic timetables so that you will maximize participation from your students and their parents.

**Newsletter**-This is necessary. Learn to plan and put your plans on paper as soon as you can. It can be monthly, bi-monthly, quarterly, or yearly, but it must include events up to a year in advance on it. Don't assume people will know if you don't tell them often. You will find an example of one and their critical elements in the Appendix.

**Postcards**-These are a great way to remind people and speak into someone's life privately. Students don't get their own mail very often. Make their day and influence a lifetime with a postcard. If you are encouraging volunteers to use them provide them with stamped, ready to go postcards.

**Website**-Keep it current, but don't expect everyone to have access to it. If you don't live in a computer literate area don't put a lot of time into this. If you do, then do it right and build a team to update it on a regular basis.

**Phone Calls**-Periodic calls and phone trees are great ways to get the word out and take advantage of some of the unpredictable opportunities that come your way. You can use lots of staff here and even another leader to maximize it.

**E-mail**-Make sure you answer it and enjoy the benefits of instant communication. If you don't plan to give quick response and answers, then don't advertise it as instant information.

**Flyers and Handouts**-Make sure they are available months in advance and on a regular basis so that even late comers can catch up and go. If your group turns them into paper airplanes, then hand them out at the end of your gatherings and mail to all when they are important.

**Personal Visits**-When it is a key event don't miss out on a personal visit. You can answer all the questions for the thousandth time and leave information behind with them.

**Drama Advertisements**-Have your drama group put together a series of creative skits that tell the rest of the group what you have coming up.

**Answering Machine Information**-If you can arrange for a dedicated line, you can have a message board that constantly updates people with the latest and most current events in the youth ministry world. It can also inform parents if you are going to be getting back later from an event than originally planned.

**Public School Newspaper Ads**-They are usually cheap, happy to take your money and a great way to get on to any campus.

**Local Radio Spots**-This can be a community or school radio station. It can be free or have a small fee. Either way, have your students produce it.

**Student Testimonies**-This is probably the best advertisement you can have. When a student tells why they are going on an event and what it did for them the last time they went you have just passed all the cultural barriers and have gone straight to a student's heart. Don't always use the same student and don't worry about the level of polish they may possess. They can say it half as well as you do but it will go twice as far.

**CD/DVD Handouts**- Put a ton of information on a CD/DVD and give it away to visitors or parents. Make a specific CD/DVD for a big event and then use the material on it as a part of your promotion materials to get good use out of the effort.

**Power Point**- Use these as students are entering the gatherings to give them the information they need in yet another way.

As you develop the greatest thing on earth--communicate. You can never over-communicate. There are two principles that you will need to understand in order to see your efforts maximized.

First, the smaller the boat the quicker the change. Don't lose people overboard. As you start, it is easy to make changes because you are small and can tell everyone. Make sure people aren't missed or told at inconvenient times. It's your job to make sure that they hear.

Second, the bigger the boat the slower the change. Don't lose people over expectations. Teams that used to be small are especially prone to this. As things grow, change will be slower in coming. If people expect to see quick change, like it used to be, they will be disappointed and potentially leave. Constantly inform them of change that is taking place, even though it may be hard to see.

For example, growth goals of twenty percent are easy to see in a group of twenty, only four new people. Growth goals of twenty percent in two hundred are almost invisible. It's already a crowd. Few would accurately notice a change in either direction.

Communication continues to advance in methods, speed, and ease. I started youth ministry with rub on letters and taped clip art. It often took four hours to produce a black and white flyer. Now four hours can produce an incredible power point presentation, a great flyer, and a website update.

As fascinating as all the new things are, there are more yet to come. Stay flexible and adaptable to the latest tools. Temporary tattoos may replace flyers and your church may have its own TV station soon.

 **Financing the Race**

*Seek first his kingdom and his righteousness and all these things will be added to you.  Matthew 6:33*

You pursue God's challenges even if you don't have the resources on hand to do it.  This is the first area of challenge that everyone faces when it comes to any kind of work for the Kingdom of God.  Most things cost money and most people pay to do it instead of getting paid to do it.  Therefore, when anything has a price tag on it people panic.  This is often the first place where people quit before they start.  Jesus was aware of the real issues so He put the challenge in a context of "doubt."

*Then the disciples went up onto the mountain where Jesus had told them to go.  When they saw Jesus, they worshipped him, but some doubted.  Then Jesus said, 'All authority has been given to me. Therefore go and make disciples of all nations baptizing them in the name of the Father and of the Son and of the Holy Spirit, teaching them to obey everything I have commanded you. And I will never leave you nor forsake you.' Matthew 28:16-20*

Those doubters found out that they were never alone. Jesus sent them all over the world and they changed it forever. You will face the same situation with your ministry students. Doubt will ooze out of their pores. Their parents will sweat financial doubt drops. Nevertheless, the stories will begin to be written as God provides and their doubt begins to go.

For other areas where finances are a part of planning then you need to learn to progress on the **no money, slow money**, and **go money**-planning system. For example, you have a God given desire to see a van purchased for the church. You could use it and so could the church, BUT the issue of money is the reason the church doesn't have one.

**No money** says you can still check on prices of new and used. You can still check on insurance premiums and the requirements for a license. You can even do some window-shopping and find out what realistic prices are. To take it a step further, you could even approach people about the prospect of donating a van.

**Slow money** means you can realistically start to look. If the church is open to financing, maybe you have a down payment. You may not have a lot but if you are faithful with it, you will be surprised at how far it goes. Since you will have already done your homework you will wisely spend any money that you do have. Too often if we don't have a plan for money it slips through our fingers like water.

**Go money** means you can do whatever you like. Make sure you do what is right and it will stand the scrutiny of the entire church. If you spend it wisely, you will have the opportunity to spend it again. If you do not, it could be a long time until you see it anymore, let alone get to spend it. That is why it is good to work through the progression of planning that the *no money-slow money-go money* reality provides.

*His master replied, 'Well done, good and faithful servant! You have been faithful with a few things; I will put you in charge of many things. Come share in your master's happiness!' Matthew 25:21*

Here is an example of how to run the same event a variety of different economic ways.

**Fun Frenzy**-You don't have any money nor do your students. However, you need time with them to develop relationships and minister to your distracters and deciders. Develop the night's activities and then ask for donations from the congregation.

**Activity One** is bowling with balls and pins from the local dollar store. You ask for five sets and then have five lanes that bowl simultaneously, assuming you have the hall space-therefore no gutter balls. Make it more difficult by having them bowl blindfolded or backwards.

**Activity Two** is the free paint balls substitute. Contact your local produce department in the grocery store(s). Old tomatoes, grapes, etc. make great paint ball substitutes. Make sure people are a safe distance away, are wearing multiple layers of old clothes and head protection

**Activity Three** is "Silent on the set, ready set, action!" Film a movie of epic proportions with a cast of "how ever many show up." Use a battle from the Old Testament, the love story of Ruth and Boaz, the treachery of David and Bathsheba including the killing of Uriah in battle, or your version of Mel Gibson's *The Passion*.

**Activity Four** is eating while viewing their production. Make up a supply list of what you would like to serve along with all the other supplies needed for the event far in advance to the congregation or donating stores.

**Activity Five** is to share Christ with everyone as the movie original is finishing up. You will have had a lot of contact time at potentially no cost to you or your students. It will also have involved the church. Now when you ask for help or prayer support the whole church will feel like they are a part of the ministry there.

**Fun Frenzy with cash.** Just do the same things you did before but take them to a real bowling alley, paint ball arena, but still shoot your movie and feed them. You can make the food creatively by having them create their own pizzas by dropping the toppings while standing on a chair. Then share the same Gospel message as they finish up the food and the movie.

One requires more work, the low cost event, while the other is more expensive. Either can work for you, it just depends on what your money options are and what your student audience is used to.

**Retreat without cash.** Stay in your own church but have people bring freestanding tents to set up for privacy and clothes changing. Make a good food list and get your donations from the church ahead of time or have people volunteer to make meals and bring them in at specific times for the main meals and snacks.

You may also be able to get food donations from local stores. Housing and food are usually your two biggest expenses.

From that point, pick any of the retreats in the target section and see what supplies they require and look for donations for those as well.

If you have money then you can do just about anything, anywhere. But don't let money fool you into thinking things will work just because you can throw money at an issue or event. You still need to pick targets and plan to hit them with your ministry efforts.

**Youth Center for your community without cash.** When you don't have any money you need to do what you can that doesn't cost anything. You do your homework and research on the zoning, building costs, staffing needs, and ongoing maintenance costs.

Take the time to talk to a number of successful youth centers and learn from their efforts. Make friends in that world so you can talk to them at any critical stage along the way.

If you have done your homework well then when you do get some money, slow money, you will spend it wisely since you already have a plan. Well-spent money draws more money. Faithful with a little means you will be faithful with more. In time, you can have a youth center for your community even though your original vision didn't have any cash to start with.

Your financial status shouldn't determine what you do just how you do it. Never let money be an excuse for what you do or don't do. If you do then you will spend the rest of your life bowing to it instead of the one we are reminded of when we spend it, "In God We Trust."

 **Painting your Grandstands**

Some of you reading this book have a real live castle where you are the only one using your great facility and it is dedicated and designed specifically for youth ministry. Others may feel like they have a dungeon or you may be in a rented facility that requires a set up and a tear down every time you want to use it.

Each situation can make you bitter or better as you learn to work with the castle that God has given you to work with for now. If you have the perfect facility, you might pick up a few pointers but this section isn't specifically for you. If not, here are some ways to make the most of your setting.

As you noticed for the majority of the classroom settings we discussed in **Training in the Classroom**, we didn't require much setup or special building use. That's because we have used rented, under construction, multiple use facilities in all of our youth ministry settings. We've never enjoyed a space dedicated to youth ministry.

When you rent but want to make the room like your own, you can use several props to do that. Banners can transform a room quickly with little effort and only a moderate start-up cost. You can also customize them if you have students or staff with an artistic bent of any kind. Often Christian book stores have posters and banners that they recycle after a selling season that you may be able to get free.

Plastic piping, as used in plumbing, can also be used to construct a backdrop at a minimal cost and need for storage. They can also double as puppet stages and other useful items in the ministry world.

If you have a room that is yours to use, also check out the bulletin board, chalk board, etc. options that exist in it. You may be able to put things up there when you meet.

Stage backdrops are painted on large canvasses stretched over lightweight frames. You can do the same thing with light wood frames and old sheets. Painted, they can be anything you want them to be. Using colored or patterned sheets can help set the stage as well. Perhaps Spiderman could be the main attraction for some students.

Banners are also readily available and can transform a room quickly. Suspended from the ceiling or hung on the wall they can put the "youth" element into the room quickly.

Each one of these requires work so don't look at it as your project but someone's project. You may need to get the creative ball rolling but someone, or a group of someone's, would probably enjoy the opportunity to be involved. If you can give some guidelines and direction then you can reap the benefit from their efforts. If you cut them loose without guidelines, then enjoy whatever they have done and make the most of it.

Having access to the same rented room every week will force creativity and flexibility. Those are both great ministry traits that you can rely on even if you end up having a room that you can call yours. Should that happen don't settle into the "same old, same old" every time. We all need to avoid that teaching trap.

If you have a room you can call your own but share it, you may still need to do everything we have already discussed or rely on some of these creative options. Perhaps each using group can have a wall that they call theirs and can leave up their distinct items. You just face a different way when you have your own setting.

If you don't have a wall then bulletin boards can be made or bought that open to reveal a lot of square footage and when closed hide it all. Our last setting utilized two large walls and bulletin boards that gave us nearly two hundred square feet of "youthisms." We could leave up things that the wedding, that weekend, didn't have to look at, because the bulletin boards closed up and covered their content.

When the room is a multiple use facility, don't be surprised by what happens when you're not there and by the blame that comes your way for things that may or may not happen when you are. Youth are known to be energetic and will sometimes be blamed for things that they couldn't have done. In all of this, just get bigger and not bitter. Growing in the grace and knowledge of our Lord and Savior Jesus Christ is a constant lesson for all of us.

Don't be afraid to abandon the facility either. You may meet there but remember you may have a great parking lot, cemetery, church bus, parking garage, mall, or restaurant near by that can become your setting for some special lessons.

You may also have some untapped square footage that is always available because no one else has seen the value in it yet. Our first meeting room was an attic. We used the low ceilings and stairs going up to nowhere to our advantage. It became our little youth shelter.

I have also met in an old garage that was renovated with junkyard parts into a very cool youth facility. The church vans still park there but they move out easily and you have space for almost a hundred students.

If you have the "Cadillac" facility don't rely on it to facilitate youth ministry. It, too, can become the "same old, same old", if you're not careful.

Your use of your facility will also be based on the size of group you are working with and the time period you have to work with. Small groups have a different dynamic than a group over one hundred. If you have forty-five minutes or two hours then you have to look at your facility in a different way as well.

Here are some helpful hints for your group size and time constraints.

With zero to five students, you need to think small group dynamics. Give people time to open up and take risks. It may also limit some of your lessons and activities. Visitors also need to be integrated as quickly as possible so they don't feel left out or awkward. Watch your students and staff because their body language will tell you a lot about the effectiveness of your small group.

In small groups like this, it is critical that you let the students develop and not be too hasty at answering your own questions or getting frustrated by a lack of participation. It also means your other staff will have to be quiet too and allow the students to become involved.

Moving to the six to twelve student size, you now have more options including breaking them down into two smaller groups for certain times. You may also divide the genders at appropriate times. Most of what you do will still be helped if you take the small group dynamics into account. You can use some help to run another group within the bigger group.

With thirteen to twenty students, you are now entering into the classroom size that students are used to. There is a definite safety level there for them but also some of the same dynamics that you may see in a school classroom, no attention from anyone. Now you have to look at a well-planned lesson or you can lose your impact in the group.

You may not know everyone in this setting and that will create the need for nametags or some way of learning new people's names. Your need for additional help increases as well because just knowing their name isn't enough to base ministry on. Someone on the leadership team needs to know every student that ever walks through your doors more than once. Three staff can each know five and you can take care of the first five visitors. Somehow, know your students.

With this size and up to the forty level, you have a classroom size that they are familiar with and can do almost anything that your space and time frame allow. Preaching, group games, multiple small groups, teaching stations where you have several activities happening all at the same time at various locations in the room, all work in this size group. It is easier to make sure everyone is involved and learning than when you take the next step and go past forty.

You can teach from the front by yourself but you will be wiser and stronger if you have a number of staff sprinkled throughout the group facilitating greeting, altar work, supply disbursing, information dispensing, media use, gathering of permission slips and cash, and any offerings you may take. With other staff in charge of other parts of a meeting, you also open the door for the students to be involved under the staff's care, not yours.

Forty to seventy requires another level of planning and recognizing some of the dynamics that a group this size generates. This size is bigger than their daily world so you may have to educate your students on how to act in it. If you don't, it is easy for one element of the group to take over and exclude or drive away others.

For example, if it is a mixed group of junior high and senior high students, often one will dominate, driving away the other. Few seniors in high school want to put up with dozens of their little brothers running around. In the other direction, few seventh graders want to have dozens of big sisters running around either. These sizes require more structure and control to keep them moving in the right direction with their dynamics.

Your involvement level by staff at this point needs to be substantial. Your students may do all the work of the evening but you need to have staff in charge of all the areas so you aren't the "go to guy" and can concentrate on the teaching, preaching, lesson, etc. for the session at hand.

Over seventy, you have stepped into the mini concert crowd. In this setting, you have to plan each gathering until you have several systems in place: greeters, offerings, announcements, multimedia, worship, drama, etc., that work no matter how you format your gathering. Remember that crowds are not good learning settings so don't base your success on how many people walk through the doors.

Disciples aren't raised in crowds. They can be called and motivated but not trained. No matter how many walk through the doors for any given session remember you are called to make disciples and reach the lost not solely entertain, motivate, or challenge students.

Your potential with the greater numbers is very high but for individual growth to happen you must have more opportunities in place than just a large group setting. That's why small groups are so important for the discipleship aspect of youth ministry.

As we examine our last major section in the text you will see how all of the issues we have mentioned come together to form a healthy youth ministry that produces disciples from your students and staff.

 **Youth Ministry Checkup Checklist**

All of this new activity has the potential of creating a very healthy youth ministry (or a Frankenstein). What that looks like will vary with each community and church. In this checklist are areas that you can evaluate to chart your progress in vital areas. See how you're doing and use the results to guide your future work with this part of the body of Christ. It should help tie together everything we have been talking about.

*A good tree cannot bear bad fruit, and a bad tree cannot bear good fruit. Matthew 7:18*

Preventive medicine is always better than corrective surgery. Eating well is always better than the results of a lifetime of poor eating habits. Never starting to smoke is always easier than stopping an ingrained habit. You get the picture.

This checklist will enable you to see how things are progressing in the youth ministry world you are a part of. It is intended to be a check up where nobody but you and God are poking around. That way you can be honest. That way you don't have to defend something or someone you may not understand anyway.

Set some time aside to do this. It asks real questions so don't rush your answers. An honest look will allow you to know your current health and how to improve it. If you start now, you can look forward to long term health.

This applies to volunteers, part-time trained professionals, or full time long-term youth staff. It applies to anyone who is working with the goal of seeing young people serve Jesus the rest of their lives.

We have tried to remove any bias that may exist due to region, culture, church size, or the amount of time available for youth ministry. In short, this will have an application wherever you are ministering.

Once you have done the initial checklist then chart out any course of change that is needed. Your personal ministry health and the health of the ministry you are a part of depends on it. Don't wait until you have a crisis to look for the cure. Start now. Truth sets you free if you apply it.

You will see many areas covered by this checklist. Youth ministry isn't accomplished with five key steps or nine programs. It is an organism, the body of Christ. There are a lot of factors that determine the long-term health of a youth group. Because there are so many factors, you can have a youth ministry that is growing and still not have one that is healthy. In the same sense you can have one that isn't growing yet but is healthy and will grow in time. Look and learn.

The Gospel produces healthy people and groups.  Your capacity to work alongside the Gospel and the Father, Son, and Holy Spirit will determine the ultimate strength, size, and health of your group.

## What is a healthy youth ministry anyway?

A healthy youth group isn't determined by a certain size. It isn't determined by how many people are receiving Christ each month. Nor is it determined by any one factor you can determine quickly.

Healthy youth groups begin with what they have, individually and corporately, as they grow towards the life that Jesus gave us to live. If we live that life, as individuals and a group, it will in time produce others who will do the same-- disciples.

When that happens is dependent on the spiritual condition of the people in your particular area and the past work of others. If your area has had generations of good watering, prayer, planting, and sharing of God's truth and love through deed and word, then you may have the privilege of harvesting a large number in a short time. If no one has worked there before you, then you have a lot of unseen work to do.

You may live in an area where:

- There is a heavy influence from a church that isn't Christian.
- The last youth worker may have slept with a student or stolen money.
- Your community may be known for its huge transitory welfare population.

All of these factors can slow the progress of your efforts.

Typically, a youth group that is only maintaining its population will have up to about ten percent of the church population. In a church with a thousand on a Sunday morning, having one hundred students may just be maintenance and not growing at all. On the other hand, if the one thousand are all over sixty in age, then that one hundred could be a very healthy and vibrant group.

You can't pin them down except to look at the health indicators. This is no time to try to polish a trophy. It's just a time to look and learn. Growing people make a growing, healthy youth group possible. Let's see how it works.

## Scoring the Questions

To come away with any kind of understanding of the health factors we have established a rating scale. Each level is explained and given a number value. They are as follows:

0- Wasn't aware of the issue and haven't addressed it. Taking this checklist brought this area to your attention.

2- We are in the early stages of frustration in this area. You aren't sure where to turn or what to do about this one but you are aware of it.

4- We are experimenting with this area. You have begun to try and install some kind of health factor in this area.

6- This area is stable. You have some mechanism or person that is helping this to work at this time.

8- This area is stable and growing. You have a mechanism or person that is proving to work consistently and with increasing health.

10- This area is flourishing. You are reaping the results of an established integral part of the youth ministry.

As you can see, there can be a large spread between points. Good. That will allow you to see where you still have some work in front of you. Work is always involved where change and growth are involved.

It is good to average a seven or better for each area in order to see health as a long-term reality. Any areas below that level aren't healthy for the long term even if the group has grown in numbers. Address those areas with the lowest numbers first in the order of importance. For example a low score in the skeletal area needs attention before a low score in the skin does. A low score in the muscle area needs attention before one in the hearing area.

Each area is critical but just as in first aid you have to stop the bleeding before you can fix the broken leg. You will also have to look at areas you can accomplish while you are waiting for opportunities to work on the others. For example, you may not have any staff right now. Until you get some you can't work specifically on an area. You can prepare for the time when you will have them but until then you can address other areas.

Don't stop doing what has been done to help one area at the expense of another. The last section can help you to chart change and see a healthier ministry develop.

Christ calls His church the Bride. Getting her ready for the Bridegroom is our goal. Learn from the checklist. Chart your course and get ready for the wedding!

## Skeletal Structure

| 0 | Wasn't aware of the area |
|----|---|
| 2 | Frustrated here and not taking action yet |
| 4 | Experimenting here |
| 6 | Stable, it is working okay |
| 8 | Stable and growing positively |
| 10 | Flourishing and we are reaping the benefits |

Just how big and strong you get is dependent on four basic traits in your youth ministry setting.  Of primary importance is the personal growth of the key leader.  Are they growing in all the areas that life throws at them?  Like Christ's house built on the rock (Matthew 7:24-28), any youth minister must have Christ's teachings as the core of their personal life.  Ministry brings in the rain, wind, and rising waters at a sometimes alarming rate.  Here are some areas that need to be explored.  If you are the primary leader how are you doing?

☐ Is your relationship with God solid and challenging?

☐ How about the relationships you have with those in authority over you?

☐ Are your finances disciplined and stable?

☐ How is your spouse doing?

☐ Is your family growing in their spiritual lives?

☐ Are you growing in God's area of calling in your life?

If these are solid then you have something to pass on to others.  As a leader, you must pass on life skills not just how to preach a good sermon.  If you aren't the primary leader then how can you help them to succeed in these areas?  All of life has to be stable and growing in order for a youth ministry leader to be long term and fruitful.

Good sermons and ministry skills are important and they are the second areas of growth.  Are you growing in your ministry skill levels and areas?  Or are they the same as they were a few months or years ago?  If you aren't involved in these areas, is someone properly trained and supported there?

☐   Sermons

☐   Teaching

☐   Counseling

☐   Parent Meetings

☐   Staff Training

☐   Discipleship

☐   Evangelism

☐   Hospitality

☐   Follow-up

☐   Campus Ministry

☐   Worship

☐   Administration

☐   Marketing

Number three of the big four areas of skeletal development is the training of your staff people.  You can't disciple more than a few students at a time. Somewhere in your efforts must be the equipping of additional leaders. To have a strong, long-term, healthy ministry you need about one leader for every four students you are working with. Basic math says that you probably need more than you have and if you're looking at numerical growth and health then you will always be training those you have and have a system in place to train the newer leaders that must come alongside.

☐    Do you have consistent training times?

☐    Do you have a system to train new leaders?

☐    Do you have leaders working in areas of gifting and calling?

☐    Do you have a functioning communication system that keeps them informed and abreast of the ministry issues?

☐    Are you developing other leaders to replace you in a variety of areas?

For the final area of skeletal development, let's look at the students that you are ministering to. Do they have the opportunities to grow in the levels of involvement that Christ calls them to?

This means, from their beginning steps as pre-Christians to the leadership steps that budding full time ministers need to take, that they can count on training and opportunities to grow in their faith just like you get. Do they have opportunities in the following times of their lives?

☐    Pre-Christian exploration time

☐    New believers basics training

☐    New believers ministry involvement- not the same things as more mature believers

☐    Ministry opportunities that are consistent with the variety of gifts. This should be a large proportion of your yearly calendar

☐    Full time ministers ministry training track

☐    Missionary training track

☐    Vocational Christian ministry track

As you can see, this is a lot of work. It is another reason why you need so many co-laborers. The number of your co-laborers determines your size. It also determines how much muscle you can eventually have which eventually determines the long term health. Much is determined by these four factors and missing any one of them will limit what can be done in your situation.

Temptation comes when you realize that your personal growth and the growth of the staff are all unseen labor. People see your ministry skills and those of your students. They will pat you on the back for them. But you won't last long if you don't take the time to work behind the scenes and grow personally and corporately with the people God has given you to work with.

Total Scores _____ divided by thirty-one equals_____

# Muscle

| 0 | Wasn't aware of the area |
|----|---|
| 2 | Frustrated here and not taking action yet |
| 4 | Experimenting here |
| 6 | Stable, it is working okay |
| 8 | Stable and growing positively |
| 10 | Flourishing and we are reaping the benefits |

Muscles only come about by work, work, work, and more work in new ways. Here are the four key muscle development techniques that work alongside the skeletal development. If you are growing both at the same time, they influence each other's development. If your muscles are growing and developing, they can increase the ultimate skeletal structure's size.

First is the area of **evangelism**. Biblical evangelism always begins with the "leave it all behind" message of repentance. If students aren't challenged to the full message, you won't see the full results. You can't toss Jesus into their mess and see life changing results unless they give Him their lives to change.

☐   Is repentance a part of the invitation that you extend to the lost?

☐   Is repentance a part of the lifestyle believing students and staff practice?

☐   Do people understand repentance well enough to share it in their message to the lost?

☐ Is the rest of your ministry consistent with the original "leave it all behind" call in the opportunities that are given to the students?

Next is the area of **equipping**. Are students and leaders equipped for all areas of life? Very few people are equipped in all the areas that life throws at them. Few families and fewer individuals have the capacity to give a solid foundation to anyone. You need tools for every area of life or they will be your downfall.

You need to work in harmony with families but not in ignorance of their capacity to do their job. Most parents are giving it their best efforts. Help whenever and however you can. Investing in parents will pay some of the highest dividends you can possible get. Are there opportunities for the following areas?

☐ Loving God basic training

☐ Loving people basic training

☐ Basic apologetics-defending their faith in light of science, current events, and religion

☐ Finances

☐ Decision-making

☐ Anger and conflict

☐ Thought life

☐ Bible study methods

☐ Ministry tools

**Encouragement** needs to be a fiber that runs through out the muscle tissue. Developing new muscle is tiring and doesn't happen over night. It is easier to quit than to continue. It is easier to look at the failures than the future. Hebrews 3:13 reminds us that it needs to be a daily event.

☐  Is everyone encouraged to new levels of participation?

☐  Are failures viewed as never fatal but only stepping-stones to new skills?

☐  Is encouragement given to all people at all levels?

☐  Does everyone rejoice with those who rejoice and mourn with those who mourn?

☐  Is encouragement expressed through more than just verbal messages-notes and awards?

☐  Do you celebrate the achievements of your students through special events?

These **evangelized, equipped, and encouraged** students and staff will need places and opportunities of **employment** in the Kingdom of God. How to keep all these student saints moving forward can be your biggest challenge.

☐  Do you provide opportunities for the new student?

☐  Do you provide opportunities for the established student?

☐  Do you provide opportunities for those called to church related ministry?

☐    Do you provide opportunities for those called to missions?

☐    Do you provide opportunities for those called to mercy ministries?

☐    Do you provide opportunities for those called to helps ministry?

☐    Do you provide opportunities for those who are called to a vocational Christian life?

☐    Do you provide opportunities for those with special needs and personal limitations?

☐    Do you provide opportunities in a timely manner?

☐    Do you provide growing opportunities for your new staff?

☐    Do you provide growing opportunities for your established staff?

Total Scores _____ divided by thirty equals _____ .

## Skin

| 0 | Wasn't aware of the area |
|----|--------------------------|
| 2 | Frustrated here and not taking action yet |
| 4 | Experimenting here |
| 6 | Stable, it is working okay |
| 8 | Stable and growing positively |
| 10 | Flourishing and we are reaping the benefits |

Skin holds it all in. It gives you the distinctive of the location and the people that make up your expression of the body of Christ. Like any area of your body, it can be healthy or sickly. These four key issues are often overlooked but they can never be ignored.

Are your students **culturally relevant** or are they culturally contaminated. Romans 12:2 calls us to be transformed by the renewing of the mind. In that change we still need to be able to maintain an audience with the lost. There is a danger of becoming a club that has an exclusive membership and language.

☐ We use a vocabulary that is easily understood by all.

☐ Our topics are relevant to the issues of everyday life.

☐ Lost people recognize our sincerity and genuine efforts.

☐ Our community knows who we are.

☐ Our schools know who we are.

☐ Our jails know who we are.

Socially we have tried to eliminate the differences between Adam and Eve. Biblically you dare not do that in youth ministry. You must recognize, understand, and program accordingly to see both genders flourish.

☐ Do you have separate events for the two genders?

☐ The two genders do not compete against each other.

☐ Is each gender given the opportunity to succeed independently of the other?

☐ Does each gender have key leaders that are competent in gender specific issues and available to the students?

Given the variety of people that God has created, it becomes a challenge to help them work together and find their place in the body of Christ. If they are given the truth of who they are and how others are different, they can function with a lifetime of service.

Spiritual, motivational, and personal gifts are like diamonds in the rough. Each one starts in an immature form. However, given an understanding of the gift and its place in the kingdom, each student can flourish.

☐ Does each student have the opportunity to find his or her gifts?

☐ Does your staff have the opportunity to find their gifts?

☐ Is each gift honored and utilized?

☐ Does each student have the opportunity to mature in his or her gifts?

☐ Does your staff have the opportunity to mature in their gifts?

☐    Does each student have the opportunity to learn how to cooperate with those that have other gifts?

☐    Does your staff have the opportunity to learn how to cooperate with those with other gifts?

All of these issues come down to the point of the effectiveness of your method with the students you have, not the ones you wish you had or have had in the past.    Is it all talk or do they get the opportunity to grow in their faith and ministry skills?

☐    Do new converts get the opportunity to exercise their faith where their failures are not critical?

☐    Do students have the opportunity to exercise their faith at any level of their spiritual maturity?

☐    Do your discipleship methods take into account the variety of backgrounds that your students have?

Total Scores _____ divided by twenty equals _____

## Coordination

| 0 | Wasn't aware of the area |
|---|---|
| 2 | Frustrated here and not taking action yet |
| 4 | Experimenting here |
| 6 | Stable, it is working okay |
| 8 | Stable and growing positively |
| 10 | Flourishing and we are reaping the benefits |

Coordination is not an automatic in anyone. It comes as all the body parts work in cooperation with each other and is the same in any youth ministry. You can do a lot right BUT if you miss the coordination factor, you can find yourself stumbling through opportunities instead of being able to take full advantage of them. You may also find yourself at odds with other parts of the body of Christ. Unity doesn't exist under those conditions and neither does Christ's blessing.

The first area of coordination is your ability to work with the whole **church calendar**. There is life outside of youth ministry. You must work within that framework to be a happy and healthy part of your local church.

☐ Do you plan the use of your local facility in cooperation with the rest of the church departments?

☐ Are your students involved in the other departments of your church in ministry?

☐ Is your youth ministry mission statement in harmony with the overall church mission statement?

☐    Do you utilize the existing church communication tools?

☐    Do you use your areas of expertise to better the other ministry departments?

☐    Are the big events of your local church also big events on your youth ministry calendar?

Your youth ministry is dependent and intertwined with the **local school campus calendar** in a unique way. If you don't coordinate with them you will find yourself tripping over them on a regular basis.

☐    Do you get every school event calendar as soon as it is available?

☐    Do you take advantage of the scheduled school vacation days?

☐    Do you attend school calendar events when they further your ministry purposes?

☐    Are you involved on the school campus on their calendar terms?

Stepping outside the realm of the school and the church, you need to look at your **local community calendar**. Within those dates, you may find opportunities to accomplish many of the youth ministry goals you have for your students without having to leave home.

☐    Do you obtain the community calendar at the earliest possible opportunity?

☐ Do you look for ways to further your youth ministry goals in your own community?

☐ Are you building on each year's use of the local calendar?

☐ Are you taking advantage of the local events with evangelistic efforts?

☐ Does your church participate in local church networks?

☐ Do you participate in the local youth ministry network?

☐ Are there seasonal work issues that impact your community-harvest, mill closures, fishing seasons, tourist trades, etc?

For most of us there exists a **denomination** that we affiliate with. They have opportunities that exist to further your efforts in youth ministry.

☐ Do you obtain the calendar opportunities at the earliest possible dates?

☐ Are you cooperating with those opportunities that further your youth ministry goals?

☐ Do you seek help from the denominational resources that exist for you?

Total Scores _____ divided by thirty-six equals _____

With all the great ministry plans that you have, how well do you communicate those opportunities to your students and their families? To see your students optimally involved you must inform them for each event at least six times with at least three different methods. Parents need to be informed at least three different times to effectively secure their participation and understanding.

If you are new to a situation, that number may need to actually increase whereas longevity and consistency will eventually allow you to reduce the number in some cases.

## The Growth Plate

| 0 | Wasn't aware of the area |
|---|---|
| 2 | Frustrated here and not taking action yet |
| 4 | Experimenting here |
| 6 | Stable, it is working okay |
| 8 | Stable and growing positively |
| 10 | Flourishing and we are reaping the benefits |

Growth always comes with a price tag. People make mistakes. Failure is written all over people's attempts in new areas. If there is an environment where that is accepted and understood, the body can grow. As soon as people can't grow, as ugly as that can be sometimes, the growth plate disappears and you are destined to plateau at that height.

Peter is our Biblical example of someone who grew and what it took him to do it. We can't expect it to be any easier or prettier today with your students or staff. If you aren't familiar with these scriptures make sure you take the time to look them up and study them.

☐    Are people allowed to attempt and fail in their faith attempts? (Matthew 14:22-23)

☐    Are people allowed to attempt and fail in their progress in hearing God's voice? (Matthew 16:13-23)

☐    Do people experience Biblical forgiveness in line with Biblical repentance? (Mark 14:66-72)

☐    Are students and leaders given the opportunity to grow beyond their past failures? (Acts 2:28-39)

All of this growth doesn't automatically happen. We must work alongside Father God, Jesus and the Holy Spirit and their efforts on our behalf. If we do, we will establish a training regimen that produces fruit and change in lives. Without it, we will short-circuit what God is trying to do with us, through us, and to us.

Our services, retreats, ministry times, altar sessions, and structure must encourage the following to happen. If we don't make them a part of our structure, the students and staff probably won't make it a part of their daily lives.

☐ Do people learn to respond to the prompting of the Holy Spirit? (John 16:7-9)

☐ Do people learn to enter God's presence? (John 14:6)

☐ Do people allow God to comfort their hearts? (2 Corinthians 1:3-4)

☐ Do people cooperate with God in the renewing of their minds? (Romans 12:2)

☐ Do people submit to the Lordship of Jesus Christ? (Mark 1:17)

☐ Do people walk in the power of the Holy Spirit for life's challenges? (Acts 1:8)

Total Scores _____ divided by ten equals _____

# Hearing

| 0 | Wasn't aware of the area |
|---|---|
| 2 | Frustrated here and not taking action yet |
| 4 | Experimenting here |
| 6 | Stable, it is working okay |
| 8 | Stable and growing positively |
| 10 | Flourishing and we are reaping the benefits |

The more active a body becomes, the greater the need to hear what is going on around it. Without hearing, problems occur. Fortunately, we are given a variety of sound sources that enable us to hear what we need to in order to function successfully. As leaders, we need to be able to hear the specific direction that applies to our group and we need to teach the students and staff the same skills.

☐   Do we enable people to respond to their conscience? (John 16:5-11)

☐   Do we enable people to respond to the work of the Holy Spirit? (John 16:12-15)

☐   Do we enable people to get and apply the truths of God's Word?

☐   Do we enable people to learn from God's example of creation?

☐   Do we enable people to learn from songs, hymns, and spiritual songs?

☐   Do we enable people to learn from words of wisdom?

☐    Do we enable people to learn from those in authority over us?

☐    Do we hear what donkeys have to say, for example, Balaam's donkey, those unusual sources that we don't always expect to hear from?

Total score _____ divided by eight equals _____

# Vision

| 0 | Wasn't aware of the area |
|----|--------------------------|
| 2 | Frustrated here and not taking action yet |
| 4 | Experimenting here |
| 6 | Stable, it is working okay |
| 8 | Stable and growing positively |
| 10 | Flourishing and we are reaping the benefits |

Without vision, a body loses many of the opportunities it would have otherwise had. Vision for any part of the body of Christ is dependent on several things.

☐ Do people see Jesus? (Hebrews 12:2)

☐ Do people walk in grace? (1 Corinthians 15:9-11)

☐ Do people give and receive mercy? (Hebrews 4:16)

☐ Do people understand biblical faith? (Hebrews 11)

☐ Do people seek the truth and its consequences? (John 8:31-32 & Hebrews 12:11)

☐ Do people understand the battle realities? (Ephesians 6)

☐ Do people see other people the way God does? (Ephesians 6:12)

☐ Do people know how to view their past?

☐ Do people know how to view their present?

☐ Do people know how to view their future?

Total score _____ divided by ten equals _____

## Reaction Time

| 0 | Wasn't aware of the area |
|----|---------------------------|
| 2 | Frustrated here and not taking action yet |
| 4 | Experimenting here |
| 6 | Stable, it is working okay |
| 8 | Stable and growing positively |
| 10 | Flourishing and we are reaping the benefits |

Get out of the way. Move your hand out from under the hammer. Put the brakes on before you get to the stop sign. These are all indicators of our reaction time. For a special driver's license that I needed in order to drive a school bus, I had to pass a test that showed my reaction time was up to the new level of responsibility. As we grow and go, we will need to sharpen our reaction time.

Without a good reaction time, we are destined to heartache and trouble. With it, we will miss a truckload of trouble that we never saw coming. Here are some of the key areas to examine our reaction time.

☐ How do we obey when working with new things?

☐ How do we obey when working with old things?

☐ How do we obey when working with easy things?

☐ How do we obey when working with difficult things?

☐ How do we obey when working with humbling things?

☐ How do we obey when working with those in authority?

Total score _____ divided by six equals _____.

# Endurance

| 0 | Wasn't aware of the area |
|---|---|
| 2 | Frustrated here and not taking action yet |
| 4 | Experimenting here |
| 6 | Stable, it is working okay |
| 8 | Stable and growing positively |
| 10 | Flourishing and we are reaping the benefits |

Endurance is the ability to take your body to and through the next steps of life. "Looking Good" doesn't mean anything if you can't walk the talk. These are the issues that will impact the area called endurance. It takes time to get it and time to have it tested and proven. None of those are easy or necessarily fun. Nevertheless, if we have them we have a greater capacity for life than anyone else does.

☐ Do we provide discipleship so people can love God in all areas of life?

☐ Do we provide discipleship so people can love people in all areas of life?

☐ Do we provide discipleship so people can succeed in all areas of ministry?

Discipleship forces apologetics. The deeper you go into the ways of God the deeper you must go into God Himself. He does just fine with the deeper exploration but we don't always do it. If we don't, we will see unanswered questions become stumbling blocks instead of paving stones for the future of students and staff.

☐    Do we provide apologetics so people can love God in all areas of life?

☐    Do we provide apologetics so people can love people in all areas of life?

☐    Do we provide apologetics so people can succeed in all areas of ministry?

☐    Culture versus commands, do people do what they do because of Christ or culture?

☐    Does the group exhibit social maturity when they are together at the church?

☐    Does the group exhibit social maturity with other generations and genders?

☐    Does the group exhibit social maturity outside the church?

☐    Does the group exhibit social maturity with the lost?

☐    Does the group exhibit social maturity with other believers?

Total  Scores _____ divided by twelve  equals _____

## The Digestive Tract

| 0 | Wasn't aware of the area |
|---|---|
| 2 | Frustrated here and not taking action yet |
| 4 | Experimenting here |
| 6 | Stable, it is working okay |
| 8 | Stable and growing positively |
| 10 | Flourishing and we are reaping the benefits |

Eating is a necessary part of life. In fact, the more you do with life outside of your normal setting the chances of increasing your consumption and variety go up. We must learn how to eat in a variety of settings and situations. If we do not we won't have the quick energy we need to do the everyday things of life, let alone face the crises that life guarantees.

☐ Are you creating fussy eaters, those who can only listen to a certain style of preaching or teaching, usually yours?

☐ Meal plans, do people have a personal, regular, healthy eating schedule from the word?

☐ Gag reflex, if they eat something that is bad do they throw it up and out?

☐ Do you feed them from the full buffet of God's word or only from what's easy to prepare or your favorite dishes?

☐ Are they always hungry or are they content with what they know?

☐ Healthy bowel movements, shedding the waste products of life is a needed part of life. Do they have a mechanism to do that?

Included in the internal organs are those that draw the pollutants out of the system. They aren't pretty organs but we die without them. The liver, kidneys, and others fall into this category. They are no less essential in the body of Christ.

☐   Do people have regular opportunities to confess and forsake their sin?

☐   Do people have regular opportunities to deal with their thought life?

☐   Do people have opportunities to cleanse their hearts, hands, and homes?

☐   Do people have opportunities to mend relationships and maintain unity?

Total Scores _____ divided by ten equals _____

# Heart

| 0 | Wasn't aware of the area |
|----|----|
| 2 | Frustrated here and not taking action yet |
| 4 | Experimenting here |
| 6 | Stable, it is working okay |
| 8 | Stable and growing positively |
| 10 | Flourishing and we are reaping the benefits |

Beyond endurance is the heart that beats in any human or body of Christ. This is developed as the personal aspects of an individual's life come into perspective. If they are strong and developing, they can motivate a person to keep moving forward no matter what the obstacles. Without it, too many give up too soon and never see the results in life or ministry that the Gospel produces.

☐ Do people have the opportunity to learn and live their personal calling?

☐ Do people have the opportunity to overcome their personal challenges?

☐ Do people have the opportunity to find and develop their personal gifts?

☐ Do people have the opportunity to deal with their personal backgrounds?

☐ Do people have the opportunity to develop their own personal networks?

☐ Do people have the opportunity to passionately express their worship to God?

☐     Do people have the opportunity to pray for extended periods?

☐     Do people have the opportunity to give sacrificially to Christ's causes?

Total score _____ divided by eight equals _____

# Ribcage

| 0 | Wasn't aware of the area |
|---|---|
| 2 | Frustrated here and not taking action yet |
| 4 | Experimenting here |
| 6 | Stable, it is working okay |
| 8 | Stable and growing positively |
| 10 | Flourishing and we are reaping the benefits |

Having a fragile heart forces another issue. Most heart issues can't be addressed in a large group context. Instead, they are best nurtured in small groups. In one respect, small groups are those protected areas, like the ribcage that protects the human heart, where people all have names and everyone can honestly know each other.

Here are some areas that need a small group's safety. There is no one way to do small groups. How you do it isn't as important as the fact that each student and staff has a place where they can work on heart issues, a protected place.

☐ Do small groups exist for new staff?

☐ Do small groups exist for existing staff?

☐ Do small groups exist for new students to join?

☐ Do small groups exist for the men by age group?

☐ Do small groups exist for the women by age group?

☐ Do small groups exist for the crisis student?

☐ Do small groups exist for parents?

☐    Do your short term mission groups function as small groups?

☐    Do you have seasonal small groups for the seasonal student or staff?

☐    Do your ministry teams function as small groups?

Total score _____ divided by ten equals _____

## Crisis Capacity

| 0 | Wasn't aware of the area |
|----|----------------------------|
| 2 | Frustrated here and not taking action yet |
| 4 | Experimenting here |
| 6 | Stable, it is working okay |
| 8 | Stable and growing positively |
| 10 | Flourishing and we are reaping the benefits |

Crisis is a part of life. Each experience can be one that you grow from or one that can destroy individuals as well as the corporate body of Christ. Most of us know someone who has not dealt well with a crisis and it became their entire life instead of just a paragraph or chapter.

A good ribcage system can minimize the impact a crisis has. In those safe settings, there exists a natural group to care. Learning how to deal with these issues is an ongoing training process. Do you have one in place?

☐ Do you have people who can work with young men through their crisis issues? (Ephesians 4:26-27-Anger, Etc.)

☐ Do young men have opportunities to get equipped for their crisis issues before they become problems?

☐ Do you have people who can work with women through their crisis issues? (John 4:1-29-Relationships)

☐ Do young women have opportunities to get equipped for their crisis issues before they become a problem?

☐ Do you have people who can help families deal with their crisis issues? (Mark 5:1-19)

☐    Do you equip students to deal with the crises that exist perpetually in our world? (Matthew 24)

☐    Does staff have avenues to receive help for their crisis

Total score _____ divided by seven equals _____

## Adrenal Gland

| 0 | Wasn't aware of the area |
|----|----|
| 2 | Frustrated here and not taking action yet |
| 4 | Experimenting here |
| 6 | Stable, it is working okay |
| 8 | Stable and growing positively |
| 10 | Flourishing and we are reaping the benefits |

This little gland makes a big difference in the human body as well as the body of Christ. It represents the capacity to activate the body to action. In the spiritual body, it is too often connected to our concept of money. If we have it, we are happy to do all kinds of things. If we do not have it, we assume it can't be done.

A properly functioning adrenal gland helps the body to make progress no matter what kind of financial situation you find yourself in.

☐    When no funds are available, do you still do as much research, planning, and praying as you can about the project?

☐    When some funds are available, do you have adequate plans in place so that the money is spent wisely and in pursuit of the project?

☐    When all necessary funds are available, do you stick to your plans and see the project through to completion?

☐    Do you make decisions based on faith that God spoke to you or finances; what you can count and see?

☐    Can you account for all monies spent?

☐    Could you help others plan and prepare for their projects from God?

Total score _____ divided by six equals _____

## Danger Symptoms

| 0 | Wasn't aware of the area |
|---|---|
| 2 | Frustrated here and not taking action yet |
| 4 | Experimenting here |
| 6 | Stable, it is working okay |
| 8 | Stable and growing positively |
| 10 | Flourishing and we are reaping the benefits |

These are some of the symptoms that spell danger in any youth ministry setting regardless of group size. Outsiders who are observing the group often see them very quickly while those closest to the youth ministry may not see them. You may want an outsider to help answer these questions. Each one is the basic question, "Do you see these traits in this group?

☐   Pride

☐   Rebellion

☐   Jealousy

☐   Greed

☐   Selfishness

☐   Inhospitable

☐   Unbelief

☐   Immorality

☐   Lust:  too much, too soon, too fast, too often

☐   Lazy

☐    Sarcasm and cynicism

☐    Dishonesty

Total score _____ divided by twelve equals _____

    Each one of these is the result of some other area of neglect but they do mean something is wrong somewhere. Look it over and make the necessary changes. A thorough examination will save you volumes of heartache and trouble. Don't miss the benefits of a healthy youth ministry.

## The Prognosis and Treatment Plan

| 0 | Wasn't aware of the area |
|---|---|
| 2 | Frustrated here and not taking action yet |
| 4 | Experimenting here |
| 6 | Stable, it is working okay |
| 8 | Stable and growing positively |
| 10 | Flourishing and we are reaping the benefits |

Look at each one of the areas that the checklist has covered. For ease of treatment go ahead and put the averages for them here. For your convenience, the page numbers for the averages is listed.

☐ Skeletal Structure *page 283*

☐ Muscle *page 287*

☐ Skin *page 290*

☐ Coordination *page 293*

☐ Growth Plate *page 296*

☐ Hearing *page 298*

☐ Vision *page 299*

☐ Reaction Time *page 300*

☐ Endurance *page 302*

☐ Digestive Tract *page 304*

☐ Heart *page 306*

☐ Ribcage *page 308*

☐    Crisis Capacity *page 310*

☐    Adrenal Gland *page 312*

☐    Danger Symptoms *page 314*

An average of 0-5 in an area is reason for concern and should place this area near the top of a priority list. Areas in the 5 to 7 range need work but may work for now. Areas with a 7 or greater may be healthy enough to help pull the other areas along for a while. They can't be counted on to do it forever if the other areas are ignored.

By identifying the weak areas, you have taken the first step to health. Next, you need to make quantifiable goals. For example, if you haven't had a staff meeting in three months, schedule one for two weeks and then put them on the calendar every two weeks for the next three months.

If you haven't put together an annual calendar, then make it your goal in the next two weeks of getting all the necessary information together so you can. Have a finished calendar within a month.   These are examples of quantifiable goals. Without some way to measure success in your treatment, it is too easy to give up and just go back to the way it was.

If you are a volunteer and you lead this ministry, your progress may be slower than someone who has more time to devote to the treatment process, but maybe not. Smaller boats turn much quicker than bigger ones do. Size isn't necessarily for you or against you.

It becomes the basic practice of prioritizing, getting a plan, planning to work, and working the plan. Then check the results and modify the plan as needed. Just don't stop working.

Until you put something on a calendar and follow through on it, you are just dreaming, not making progress.

When possible take advantage of your strengths to address your areas of weakness. For example, if you are doing a good job of communication and coordination then let your needs be known, with that great tool of communication and coordination you have, and you may find there are people just waiting to fill the gaps and become part of the ministry.

If your strength is found in your muscles maybe you can change one activity to information gathering for a yearly calendar, if that is an area of weakness. For me, I was not very pastoral with the students by gifting. Instead, I was pastoral with the students when they were with me on the mission trips, five a year, which were an outlet for my gift of evangelism.

For my staff, my pastoral contribution came because of my administrative gift that enabled me to meet with them regularly. It was in those regularly scheduled times that their issues could be dealt with and their challenges for growth could be met.

Once you have started to see health come to certain areas of the ministry then re-identify the weak areas and address them. Your treatment plan will continue until you have established health in all areas.

This process is perpetual. You aren't the only one who has to work on it either. As long as it gets done you are providing a healthy body that will begin to reproduce itself and generate its own healthy habits and traits.

Does it look like a black hole for energy and time? If you keep your life healthy and growing you will be able to do what is possible. That gives God the freedom to bring in more staff and do what you can't do. You will find that establishing each of these areas in a flourishing way will perpetuate healthy growth.

Growth, that in time, will be translated into numbers and stories that you will enjoy in the telling.

Don't neglect your primary areas of personal growth and health. What we have described here is true for individuals, families, youth groups, churches, para-church organizations, ministry teams, or any living, breathing expression of the body of Christ. After all, if we don't have health what do we have?

# Community Involvement

At some point, you need to explore the other ministries within your community and any existing networks. We are a part of the body of Christ and as such should be a part of the bigger community of Christ. Having said this, I am aware that there are a large variety of existing networks and sometimes the rubble from a previous one.

Having lived in the same community for over thirty years I have worked with beginning networks, been a part of booming networks, and worked with networks who were trying to define themselves again. In other communities, we have been blessed by great networks and cursed by the divisive work of some churches in communities.

Our ability to work as a team in a community is a direct reflection of the amount of work that people put into it. Nothing just happens. Kingdom communities exist if we work outside our church box and work with those who are also working towards His kingdom. You won't see all things the same way but we can all work towards students finding Christ.

That may mean applying first aid to some of the wounds of the past. That may mean asking forgiveness for attitudes and things said about other churches. It will take time. If it grows into a cohesive group of trusting youth staff, you can attempt some big things to impact your community. Without that foundation of time, your efforts will be undermined.

As an example, I have been part of community gatherings of nearly twenty-five hundred people when no single church could muster more than two hundred. Community outreaches that are truly a byproduct of a community working together multiply the fruit and the fellowship in a way that is unique to each community.

Practically, one of your areas of common ground will be evangelism. Other areas differ greatly and often only produce unnecessary tension. You can unify on a campus strategy or for some evangelistic presentations. You should be able to work together for training purposes as well. Bringing key people in to share the expertise that already exists in the community of youth staff can be fruitful as well.

# 22 Youth Ministry Scenarios, a Safe Test

In Vietnam, they found that **if** pilots could survive their first ten missions they usually made good pilots and could survive the rest of their tour of duty.  To increase the numbers who survived they would give them easy missions their first ten times.  After that, they went into the tough ones with their rookie mistakes made when it wasn't fatal.

From that concept, the Top Gun idea and several like it were developed to increase the skill of pilots before their lives were on the line.  It has greatly increased the life of pilots and their effectiveness in combat.

In vocational ministry,  eighty percent of all people who start in ministry won't be in it in five years.  If they survive those first five years then eighty percent of them will be in ministry for the rest of their lives.  Our combat is different but even more important than the pilots that defend a country.

This text and the following scenarios are here to help you get some of the first five years under your belt before your mistakes are fatal. As you take the tests don't get defensive on your answers, learn. Don't skip over the scenarios, take the time. In the first chapter of the book you learned how to use the first aid kit.

Become an expert in first aid for yourself and others. In this, the last chapter, you will have the opportunity to show you are teachable. Become an expert in that too.

I can give you example after example after example of people that I know who didn't survive their five years of the "baptism by fire" of youth ministry. Wounded, they lay along the road of life … selling cars. We want to see you make it. So make your mistakes here on the scenarios not in the church where the mercy factor may not be high.

Here are some typical youth ministry scenarios that you may encounter. As you read them, apply what you have learned so far, and pick the course of action that should be taken. After you complete each scenario, the impacts of the choices that you would see in time are given.

By trying out our knowledge here first, we can avoid the damage that poor choices can make to individuals and youth groups. Enjoy the journey of working with youth and what it takes to minister to them. A few scenarios are enclosed but more can be found at our web site www.finish-the-race.org.

In many respects, it is a marathon race that only ends when we die. However, it should be a natural death not a death that ministry causes. Enjoy the journey and finish the race in your setting.

# Scenario A

Your students come from suburban homes where only thirty percent of them will experience divorce or death with one of their parents. The high schools they attend are all over two thousand students and are successful in sports and academics. Let's apply what we have learned to these students.

1.    T or F        These students will have all the life tools they need to succeed.

2.    T or F        These students will be filled with hope and have big dreams for the Kingdom of God

3.    T or F        These students will admire their parents and try to follow in their spiritual footsteps.

4.    T or F        These students will have been raised in church all their lives and have a good solid foundation.

*(Answers  1-F 2-F, 3-F, 4-F)*

## Scenario B

You have been giving constant challenges to your students. You were even able to get a nationally recognized speaker to come in to motivate them for Christ's causes. Which of the following course of action should you take next?

A.    You have done your job. Watch and see what God does next.

B:    You need to schedule another motivational series to keep the fires going in a few months.

C:    You need to have some equipping times ready to immediately follow the challenges.

D:    You need to have some planned opportunities for the students to participate in that enables them to fulfill the commitments they made to all the motivation they received.

E:    You need to stand aside and let God work out the leadership among the youth and not get involved in that delicate process.

*(Answers C & D)*

## Scenario C

In your youth group there are fifteen students (on a good day). Almost half of them are junior high age and most of them want to come to what is offered at the church. Which of the following statements should guide you in your work with them?

A.     Don't plan events that will seem impossible for them to achieve (distribute a thousand door hangers, collect food for twenty families, or raise a thousand dollars for a worthy project).

B.     Plan events that will seem impossible for them to achieve (distribute a thousand door hangers, collect food for twenty families, or raise a thousand dollars for a worthy project).

C.     Motivate them by telling how big the youth group will be by a specific time.

D.     Feel free to schedule other personal ministry opportunities because fifteen students don't require much time or attention from you.

E.     Treat them all like family and just let them know when things are going to happen the week before.

*(Answer: B)*

## Scenario D

Your students have just had a great camp experience and seem more motivated than ever before to be at church and be involved in spiritual things. Which of the following things should you consider in the immediate future?

A:    Don't schedule anything for a while so they can get down off their camp "high" and be who they really are.

B:    Take your vacation right after camp. You deserve the break!

C:    Have part of your staff ready to equip and involve the students in a fresh surge of activity.

D:    Be ready to work with the new converts and their network of friends and family.

E:    Carefully watch the new converts to see if it sticks ... did they really accept Christ? Otherwise you may be wasting your time investing in them if you do it too soon.

*(Answers C & D)*

Remember that more scenarios can be found at www.finish-the-race.org. If you have questions please feel free to contact us via email.

# Appendix

The following items are intended to help you form some of the materials you may need for your work with students. Take enough time to customize it for your particular setting and then feel free to use it as you see fit.

We have used these in our setting but if they are legal documents then you need to check with people from your local setting to verify their usefulness to you. Thanks!

**Contents in order:**
Sample Mixing Exercise (retreats)
Mission Trip Budget
Mission Trip Set up Checklist
Sample Permission Slip
Sample Newsletter
Youth Staff Application
The Five Keys Teaching (Disciple's Retreat)
Other Resources

# Sample Mixing Exercise (Retreat)

Put the person's name after the question. The first one to get all of the questions initialed wins. You can only use one person for one question.

1. My first car cost less than five hundred dollars _____
2. I have five or more brothers and sisters (yes steps count) _____
3. .I have broken more than one bone _____
4. I had surgery before I was twelve _____
5. My grandparents were born in another country _____
6. I've worn the same pants for five days (or more) straight _____
7. I've had to call 911 before _____
8. I fell out of a tree _____
9. I've spent at least one night in the hospital _____
10. I've traveled to more than ten states _____
11. I've never been out of this state _____
12. I've eaten food that made me sick _____
13. I've thrown up in a car _____
14. I've thrown up at school _____
15. I've been threatened by with a gun or knife _____
16. I've prayed for someone that was healed _____
17. I've been on a mission trip _____
18. I have at least two living Grandparents _____
19. My favorite food is pizza _____
20. My house more than fifty years old _____

Your Name _____

## Mission Trip Budget Worksheet

| Item Costs | Items: | Per Person $ | Running Total Team Costs |
|---|---|---|---|
| *Income* | *Participants* | | |
| *Income* | *Leaders* | | |
| *Income* | *Ultimate Leader* | | |
| *Totals* | | | |
| | Pre-flight housing | | |
| | Pre-flight food | | |
| | Pre-flight transportation | | |
| | Airline | | |
| | Airport tax | | |
| | Set up trip | | |
| | Facility rental | | |
| | Paid help | | |
| | Lodging | | |
| | Meals and Water | | |
| | Administration (printing/phone/postage) | | |
| | Ministry supplies | | |
| | Gospel literature | | |
| | Insurance | | |
| | Day off | | |
| | Transportation airport-ministry-day off | | |
| | Sound systems | | |
| | Departure tax | | |
| | Team shirt(s) | | |
| | Training materials | | |
| | Missionary needs | | |
| | Boot Camp-Training Times | | |
| | Visas | | |
| | Medical supplies | | |
| | Group souvenir | | |
| | Training Materials | | |
| | *Total Costs* | | |
| | *Total Income* | | |
| | **Balance** | | |

## SET-UP INFORMATION

Question Sheet-Get this information from the missionary or pastor you will work with.

### Transportation
- airport transportation for team and luggage
- team transportation for ministry
- team transportation for shopping
- team transportation for sightseeing trips

### Meals
- meals at hotel
- meals catered
- number of meals per day
- costs
- locations

### Housing
- name of hotel
- address/phone/FAX
- contact person
- people per room in doubles, triples, quads, etc.
- charge per room per day
- is a meeting room available_____ extra cost

### Extras
- sightseeing trips
- passport/visa costs-plus where do you get them
- airport departure tax-what currency do they require

### Missionary personal needs list-things you can bring from your team to them
- husband
- wife
- children
- ministry

### Maps
- ministry teams on site
- planning maps to take back home for future planning

♦ for door to door etc.

## Money Exchange
♦ rate
♦ contact person
♦ where located
♦ what do we bring it in? VISA? Travelers Checks? Wired in ahead? Cash? Etc.

## Dress needs
♦ climate considerations
♦ casual considerations
♦ daytime ministry considerations
♦ nightly crusade considerations
♦ male/female considerations
♦ travel considerations

## Daily Schedule
♦ time differences
♦ dates
♦ how long does it take to get used to the new time zone
♦ how do you communicate with people back home because of the time zone change

## Medical Factors
♦ Emergency medical locations
♦ on-site medical considerations
♦ immunizations required
♦ immunizations suggested but not required
♦ allergies to be considered
♦ water safety
♦ emergency contact information

## Ministry teams and supplies

## Tent
♦ location
♦ cost
♦ security
♦ seating
♦ availability
♦ sound system

♦    power availability and reliability

**Medical team (contact person [in your ministry location]            )**
♦    what medical needs can we minister to
♦    what supplies are available there
♦    where will we do the medical clinic
♦    power availability and reliability
♦    local cooperation
♦    kinds of doctors?

**Drama team (contact person            )**
♦    locations for ministry
♦    sound systems
♦    power availability and reliability
♦    appropriate styles

**Human Videos (contact person            )**
♦    locations for ministry
♦    sound systems
♦    power availability and reliability
♦    appropriate styles

**Puppet teams (contact person            )**
♦    locations for ministry
♦    sound systems
♦    power availability and reliability
♦    appropriate styles

**Mime teams (contact person            )**
♦    locations for ministry
♦    sound systems
♦    power availability and reliability
♦    appropriate styles

**Sports Teams (contact person            )**
♦    locations
♦    contact people
♦    location costs
♦    trophies/awards
♦    tournament potential target people

## Choir (contact person_____)
- ◆ sound systems
- ◆ power availability and reliability
- ◆ risers
- ◆ dress considerations

## Street Witnessing (contact person_____)
- ◆ locations
- ◆ sound systems
- ◆ power availability and reliability
- ◆ tracts
- ◆ permits or permission needed

## Prayer Chain (contact person_____)
- ◆ location

## Construction Team (contact person_____)
- ◆ location
- ◆ feasibility
- ◆ power availability and reliability
- ◆ tool considerations
- ◆ materials costs

## Literature needs (contact person_____)
- ◆ invitations crusade times
- ◆ gospel street times
- ◆ follow-up materials
- ◆ other

# Sample Permission Slip

**Participation Permission and Release of Liability**

I give permission for my child, _____ (age___) to participate in:

**EVENT**

I consent and agree to indemnify and hold harmless MY CHURCH, their agents, employees, or volunteer assistants from all claims that they or I might have arising out of my child's participation in this program which is over and above that which is covered by insurance. I have explained the meaning of "hold harmless" to my child and the signature below indicates his/her agreement to do the same. It is understood that MY CHURCH and their representatives will exercise reasonable care in the supervision and safety of my child.

_____          _____
parent/guardian signature / date          child signature/ date

**EMERGENCY MEDICAL CARE AND TREATMENT**

If it should become necessary for my child to receive medical treatment for any reason, I understand that the medical insurance policy of MY CHURCH acts in a primary position only when the participant is not already covered by insurance. Consequently, I agree to submit all claims first to my insurance company and then to the insurance company of MY CHURCH. I also accept full responsibility for the cost of medical treatment for any injury suffered while taking part in the program, which is over and above that which is covered by insurance. In addition I authorize and consent to all medical, surgical, diagnostic and hospital procedures as may be performed or prescribed by a physician to safeguard my child's health and it is not advisable to take the time to contact me in advance. I waive my right to informed consent for such treatment. Moreover I understand that temporary emergency measures may be necessary to safeguard my child's health, and I do hereby authorize and request MY CHURCH personnel to administer or supervise such treatment and to do any procedure that they deem necessary until such time as my child can be safely transported to a doctor or hospital.

Child's Full Name _____ Date of Birth __/__/__

Child's Current Weight_____ Last Tetanus Shot_____

Parents Name(s) _____

Home Address_____
          Street          City          State          Zip

Home Phone _____Work Phone _____ Cell Phone _____

Insurance Company _____ (if medical coupon please attach current copy)

Policy Holder_____ Policy/Group #_____

Allergies _____

Child's Physician_____
          Name          phone

Special Medical Information

If medication can be given as needed, how close can dosages be given?_____

Please list any other special medical information/conditions _____

Prescription Name     Dosage     Reason for taking prescription

_____     _____     _____

Permission to administer pain/fever relief medications (i.e. Tylenol) ___Yes ___No

If yes, preferred medication _____ Dosage_____

X_____
     Signature          relationship to child          date          emergency phone #

# Sample Newsletter

## EASTSIDE YOUTH "U-B-1"

**PEOPLE YOU KNOW** Have you heard that Eddie Johnson was elected to the student body as the Vice President. That Nancy Wilson is now the manager at McDonalds. Joey Smith passed his drivers license test and is now LEGALLY on the road. SO far Sally, Ed, Jill, Chad, Kristy, Kyle, Fred. Max, Sean, and Mike are going to Mexico. This year we gave $1289.09 to Speed The Light. Sean's parents donated a foosball table to the group and the quarters will help us to maintain it and work towards our STL goal for this year. Pastor Tom was recently chosen to work with the school district on the curriculum for the sex education program. We had more birthdays this month then we could count so HAPPY BIRTHDAY TO Kyle, Mike, Chad, Emily, Lisa, and Alex. We are looking forwarding to getting a birthday list on everyone so make sure you sign up now for our Birthday Banner Club.

### UPCOMING DATES

May 22 All Seniors Night 7-9pm
No Cost

June 23-July 7
That Major Mexico Trip
Cost 345.oo

July 24
Waterfight Mania $2.oo
From 11am-5pm

August 5-9
Summer Camp at Lakeside
Early Registration $89.oo
Late fee is $94.oo

Last Blast Retreat
August 27-29 Cost only $19.oo

### YOU CAN CALL US
Pastor Tom's Home #
777-7777
Church M-F from 9-5
777-7733
Sally and Ted Maxwell
777-3333

### NEWS FROM THE BOOK OF ACTS CHAPTER 29
****Prayer has worked another miracle. Mary Wilcox was released from the Hospital only three days after her car accident last weekend. Doctors doubted she would recover at all let alone so quickly. Thanks from the family and Mary. She isn't up to visitors yet but loves to get mail.
****Kyle saw a miracle last week as he paid off his Mexico trip with a reward. He had turned in a purse he found three months ago. Just last week the owner was found and was SOOOOO grateful. How grateful you ask? well it was $200.oo grateful and that paid off the trip.

## Youth Staff Application

This a cover letter that actually goes before the application and should be on church letterhead.

**First Church Youth Staff Application**

We are encouraged that you have taken this step to consider working with the students here at First Church. In order to properly consider this application and know how to work together, please fill this out completely. Incomplete applications will be returned and completed applications will be processed within two weeks.

Working with students can be one of the most rewarding and challenging things you can do with your life. Each student has unique needs. Perhaps you will be used to minister to them.

Because of these unique needs and the legal challenges of working with minors there will be a background check with appropriate agencies and calls or visits with those listed as references. Please note that honesty is considered a key part of working with the students here at First Church.

Thanks for taking the first step toward helping the youth of First Church!


Lead Youth Worker


Senior Pastor

## Youth Worker Application

| |
|---|
| Full Legal Name: |
| Address: |
| Contact Numbers: |
| Home: |
| Office: |
| Cell: |
| Email: |
| Birth date  mm/dd/yy |
| Social Security Number: |
| Driver's License Number: |
| Office Use Only: Date Submitted: |
| Office Use Only:  Dates References Checked – Comments |
| Office Use Only:  Date Application Accepted/Denied/Delayed ___/___/___ |
| Office Use Only:  Date Returned |
| Please tell us why you are interested in working with the youth here at First Church: |
| Please give a brief account of your spiritual life in the last five years: |
| Please list the results of the gifting test here:<br>Evangelist<br>Prophet<br>Teacher<br>Exhorter |

| |
|---|
| Pastor/Shepherd<br>Mercy Shower<br>Server<br>Giver<br>Administrator |
| What ministries have you been involved in during the last five years?  Who was your immediate supervisor?<br>-<br>-<br>-<br>-<br>- |
| What special gifts or skills do you feel you could use in working with the youth? |
| Do you have any arrests or convictions from a legal system?  If so, could you please list them with a brief summary of the events. |
| Describe your health condition along with any allergies or prescription drugs you may be taking. |
| What hours of availability do you see yourself having for the youth ministry here?<br>Weekends<br>Weeknights<br>Sundays |

Weekly gatherings
Camps, Retreats, or Mission trips
Flexible hours
Work at home

Please describe your family history
  Your family growing up-



  Your current family-



  Any other families from previous arrangements-



Please give us three references of people you currently work with or know through involvement in this church or other organizations.
Name:
Contact Information:

Name:
Contact Information:

Name:
Contact Information:


Do you have any of the following habits? If so, to what degree?

| | |
|---|---|
| Smoking | Never / Occasionally / Weekly / Daily |
| Alcohol Consumption | Never / Occasionally / Weekly / Daily |
| Recreational Drug Use | Never / Occasionally / Weekly / Daily |
| Watching "X" Rated Movies | Never / Occasionally / Weekly / Daily |
| Purchasing Adult Entertainment Literature | |
| | Never / Occasionally / Weekly / Daily |
| Physical Exercise | Never / Occasionally / Weekly / Daily |
| Continuing Education | Never / Occasionally / Weekly / Daily |

| Devotional Scripture Reading | Never / Occasionally / Weekly / Daily |
| Personal Prayer Time | Never / Occasionally / Weekly / Daily |
| Church Attendance | Never / Occasionally / Weekly |

Church Membership

Yes at First Church / Yes at other church / No membership

Is there anything else you can think of that we should know as we consider your application to work with the students here at First Church?

I attest that the information contained in this application is true and the church has permission to do a background check and reference check.

Signature:                                    Date:

# The Five Keys

Sooner or later, you will encounter people who belong to religious groups that don't use the Bible alone to determine their beliefs. They follow someone else's teachings, interpret the Bible through their teachings, and have an unlimited range of often-changing beliefs.

Since there are so many groups, and because their teachings often change to fit the need, it is better to stick with a few fundamental issues. These will help you to help them. It is not a battle of who is right and who is wrong. It is simply another person who needs to hear the Gospel. They have already heard enough religious talk, now they need to hear enough truth to understand the Good News.

Here are key areas, no matter what their label is. Each key topic statement will be followed by an explanation of the most common cult beliefs.

**1.     They can't be honest about sin.  You can.**

*The wages of sin is death but the gift of God is eternal life in Christ Jesus our Lord.  Romans 6:23*

*If we claim to be without sin, we deceive ourselves and the truth is not in us. If we confess our sins, he is faithful and just and will forgive us our sins and purify us from all unrighteousness. If we claim we have not sinned, we make him out to be a liar and his Word has no place in our lives.  1 John 1:8-10*

Cults tend to deal with sin in one of two ways. They ignore it completely, or they try to outweigh their personal sin with their own good works. Either way it is very difficult to be honest about yourself and your eternal future.

**2.    They can't know God because they have closed Jesus as the door. You can.**

*Jesus answered, "I am the way and the truth and the life. No one comes to the Father except through me." John 14:6*

Your personal relationship with God is something to which they can't relate. They may go to church and do many of the same religious things you do, but they don't have direct access to God. They have a form of religion instead of a lifestyle.

**3.    Their books won't get them through life. Yours will.**

*Therefore everyone who hears these words of mine and puts them into practice is like a wise man who built his house on the rock. The rain came down, the streams rose, and the winds blew and beat against that house; yet it did not fall, because it had its foundation on the rock. Matthew 7:24-25*

Once you have a good grasp of the Bible and its teachings, read some of the books that others are using as a part of their religion. Those books should sadden you. Sincere believers are devoting their whole lives to the stories, directives, and rules which are so obviously the teachings of men; not the words of God.

**4.    They don't have God's daily direction. You can.**

*Whether you turn to the right or to the left, your ears will hear a voice behind you, saying, "This is the way; walk in it."* Isaiah 30:21

*But when he, the Spirit of truth, comes, he will guide you into all truth. He will not speak on his own; he will speak only what he hears, and he will tell you what is yet to come.* John 16:13

Anywhere, anytime, and in any situation, we can get God's wisdom and direction for a day. They can't. Their direction must come from other books and people in their organizations.

**5. They don't have power over the forces of darkness or death. You do.**

*For I am convinced that neither death nor life, neither angels nor demons, neither the present nor the future, nor any powers, neither height nor depth, nor anything else in all creation, will be able to separate us from the love of God that is in Christ Jesus our Lord.* Romans 8:38-39

We know that *"the one who is in you is greater than the one who is in the world."* 1 John 4:4b. The cults leave them to work out their spiritual issues all alone. Nightmares, death, and fear often dominate the cult member's life.

These key areas will give you an effective tool to share with these people. Start with your personal testimony, then build everything else on it. They need to hear the same Gospel that you did. Even if they take offense, our best method is not attack; instead we have been given another way.

*Those who oppose him he must gently instruct, in the hope that God will grant them repentance leading them to a knowledge of the truth, and that they will come to their senses and escape from the trap of the devil, who has taken them captive to do his will.  2 Timothy 2:25-26*

Other Resources by this author available by contacting
www.mstgo.com  or www.finish-the-race.org

## Youth Ministry Resources

**Building Your Youth Staff**
CD's and worksheets to enable you to create your plan of growing a healthy
youth staff to further youth ministry in your setting.

**Creating a Climate for Change**
A seven message cassette series, showing how we can create a climate for
change for our students and staff. Includes work sheets for small groups.

**Creating Controlled Chaos**
One of Mark's latest youth ministry resources will give you creative ways to
cement Biblical principles in your audience. With over 170 pages, it contains
over 50 interactive illustrations to use with your group including scriptures,
supply lists and other helps. A few examples are in this book.

**Suicide the Friend Stealer**
A proactive approach to a potentially tragic event. It equips students, staff
and parents to understand and help prevent the loss of another student from
this generation.

**Dealing with the Anger Within**
This CD/manual combination will help you resolve your personal anger and
group conflict issues. This is good training for individuals and groups.

**Painting The Two White Lines** *A Life Changing Look at the Commands
Christ Left for Us. 250 page book.*   Jesus commanded us to teach all that He
taught. Organized around the two greatest commandments (Love God and
Love People) these three page "chapterettes" help us to apply all that Jesus
commanded us to obey. There are quantity discounts available for this item.

**Training for the Altar Experience**
A booklet that offers training to equip us to work with people at the altar.

**Your Gift and the Gospel**
This is a 60 page self paced personal evangelism course. It helps you learn
the three tools we can all use plus enables you to develop skills that are
consistent with your spiritual gifts. By working at your own pace you can
prepare to meet the challenges of evangelism in the day we live

## Drama Resources

**Drama Games by Shawna Beers**
This easy to use book has 16 drama games along with at least one page per
game for coaches notes. Drama games help your people to become more
comfortable with improvising and being in front of people.

**Drama Resources:  Drama in the Ministry Tool Box Volume 3**
A collection of 30 original drama written by Mark Schaufler.  Most are short, pointed drama dealing with critical issues in the church.
**Drama in the Ministry Tool Box Volume 4**
This volume has a full section on developing a drama ministry as well as over 30 new scripts, with seasonal topics as well as 2 longer productions.  153 pages.
**Drama in the Ministry Tool Box Volume 5**
15 new scripts by Mark Schaufler and Shawna Beers cover a range of topics such as: excuses, forgiveness, unfinished business, changed lives, choices, and more!

**Short Term Mission Resources**
**Spanish Drama in the Ministry Tool Box Volume 1**
This collection of 16 drama for Spanish speaking countries will allow you to cross the cultural and language barriers and effectively minister.  Designed to be learned in less than an hour, each drama is demonstrated in a 70 minute video.
**Spanish VBS Curriculum Volume One**
We have a new VBS curriculum for Spanish/English.  Included are background information, station model and a total of 12 lessons.  Designed in groups of 3 sessions so they can flex with your ministry setting.  Supply lists included.  First Year theme- Jesus is the same Yesterday, and Today and Forever.  Second Year theme - Jesus calls us to Care.
**Prepare and Lead a Short Term Mission Adventure**
Everything you need to plan, prepare and lead a STM.  Sixty pages plus the47 page  Short Term Mission Student Preparation Manual.
**Short Term Mission Student Preparation Manual**
This preparation book prepares people for a short term mission trip.  It includes in bound form; Your Gift and the Gospel, Anger and Conflict, Altar training and other mission trip preparation.  It is 3-hole punched so you can include it in a binder.  There are quantity discounts available for this item.

# Scripture Index

6 *(299)*
6:12 *(299)*
6:16 *(12)*

**2 Timothy**
2:25-26 *(344)*
3:12 *(16)*
3:12-15 *(140)*

**1 Thessalonians**
4:3-5 *(49)*

**Hebrews**
3:13 *(286)*
4:16 *(299)*
11 *(101, 299)*
12:1-2 *(179, 299)*
12:4-13 *(160)*
12:11 *(13, 81, 299)*
12:12-13 *(16, 184)*

**James**
1:2-5 *(29, 31, 158)*
1:13-15 *(102)*
4:7 *(149, 172)*
5:13-16 *(15)*

**1 John**
1:8-10 *(341)*
1:9 *(13, 86, 157)*
2:15 *(102)*
4:1 *(40)*
4:4 *(149, 343)*

**1 Peter**
5:8 *(172, 200)*
5:8-9 *(16)*

**2 Peter**
3:18 *(32, 177, 179)*
5:5 *(25)*
5:6-7 *(26)*

**Revelation**
1:5 *(178)*
3:19-22 *(103)*

# **Bibliography**

Chapman, Gary, The Five Love Languages  (Chicago, Northfield Publishing, 1995)

Jones, Laurie Beth, Teach your Team to Fish  (New York, Three Rivers Press, 2002)

Laurent, Dr.Robert, Keeping your Teen in Touch with God (Elgin Illinois, David C. Cook Publishing, 1988)

Rydberg, Denny, Building Community in Youth Groups (Loveland Colorado, Group Publishing

www.teamministry.com

www.finish-the-race.org